An Annotated Bibliography of
MULTICULTURAL LITERATURE

Annotated by Judith L. Kollar

Illustrated by Cheryl Buhler, Sue Fullam, Keith Vasconcelles, and Theresa Wright

Table of Contents

Teacher Created Materials, Inc.
P.O. Box 1040
Huntington Beach, CA 92647
©1993 Teacher Created Materials, Inc.
Made in U.S.A.
ISBN 1-55734-372-1

Introduction

This is the great new problem of mankind. We have inherited a large house, a great "world house" in which we have to live together — black and white, Easterner and Westerner, Gentile and Jew, Catholic and Protestant, Moslem and Hindu — a family unduly separated in ideas, culture, and interest, who, because we can never again live apart, must learn somehow to live with each other in peace.

— Martin Luther King, Jr.

These powerful words appear in Dr. King's last book, *Where Do We Go from Here: Chaos or Community?* Written the year before his assassination, they ring just as true today as they did twenty-five years ago. The Los Angeles up-rising, the nation-wide increase in hate crimes, the strife in Eastern Europe, the horror in Somalia, the war in the Persian Gulf — they all testify to the fact that Dr. King's dream of a "world house" united has yet to be realized.

If we teachers who share Dr. King's dream hope to contribute to the building and maintenance of a peaceful "world house," we must get to work in our own backyards. In our spheres of influence we must build families of students who from an early age learn not merely to tolerate but to relish the racial and cultural diversity that enriches our classrooms, our schools, our neighborhoods, our towns, our states, our country, and the world at large.

How can we get started with this seemingly gargantuan undertaking? We can fill our classrooms, our school libraries, and our entire curriculum with high quality children's literature that depicts via word and illustration the world's multicultural riches, riches that for far too long have been marginalized, if not completely ignored in many American schools. In this way, we can begin to teach our children that Tuan and Lupita merit as much attention and respect as, for decades, Dick and Jane received. Even a quick perusal of the reviews comprising this annotated bibliography will reveal numerous characters who are actually much more interesting and appealing than the sanitized Dick and Jane.

With its focus on well-executed works, this bibliography is meant to provide teachers with easy access to a wide assortment of books that will not only develop students' multicultural perspectives but will also enhance literature-based studies in all subject areas and thus can be profitably integrated into existing curricula without the need for major revision or sacrificing quality. Within the following pages can be found books focused on cultures originating in all the major geographic regions of the world as well as works describing the experiences of Americans in all their multicultural variety.

Each book has been judged particularly appropriate for students at either the primary, intermediate, or challenging level; accordingly, teachers will find the annotated entry within only one of the bibliography's three main divisions. However, the titles of books that can be enjoyed by students of various ages and abilities have been listed in more than one division. The annotations, besides providing concise but informative summaries, evaluate the usefulness of each work in promoting multicultural education as well as its potential for contributing to the general curriculum.

Among the books reviewed here, there are sure to be many that would interest and educate every student fortunate enough to have a teacher dedicated to bringing multicultural literature into the classroom. Such a teacher will find the resources accompanying the bibliography a help in accomplishing this goal. In addition, the reproducible art found throughout the bibliography can be used to decorate bulletin boards or as part of student art projects designed to generate interest in multicultural literature. Though just a starting point, this book has much to offer teachers wishing to join in the effort to lay a sturdy foundation on which we can together build a well-constructed "world house."

Suggestions for Using Multicultural Literature

◆ Without fanfare, randomly add works of multicultural literature to classroom bookshelves where students can discover them on their own. In other words, rather than announcing that multicultural literature is interesting, important, or valuable, simply behave as if such books are a natural part of any well-stocked classroom. Students will soon see for themselves how multicultural books can enrich their reading experience.

◆ Help students develop a global perspective by placing a large wall map of the world in the vicinity of the classroom library. Each time students have finished reading a book, suggest that a colored thumb tack or pushpin be added to the map to indicate the location of the culture that has been explored in the book. Goals can be set to encourage students to read books focused on a wide variety of cultures. For example, each student might be asked to have at least one tack on each continent before the end of the semester.

◆ Taking into account the ethnic diversity of a particular class, supply books that will permit each student to study his or her ancestors' culture. Oral and written reports, art projects, potluck "parties," costume days, talent shows, and a variety of other activities will allow students to share what they have learned with their classmates.

Suggestions for Using Multicultural Literature *(cont.)*

◆ Add a multicultural dimension to all subject areas by fully exploring the whole range of multicultural nonfiction: books describing games from around the world can enrich physical education; biographies of artists, scientists, and musicians, as well as, authors from a variety of cultures can demonstrate that significant contributions have been made by people of all kinds; two or three social studies texts written from differing cultural perspectives will teach students that history is open to interpretation.

◆ Teach students the significance of holidays and festivals celebrated by families with origins in a variety of cultures by supplying appropriate literature at the time of year a particular holiday occurs — there are many children's books focused on celebrations.

◆ Make students aware that most Americans either are or have ancestors who were immigrants by exposing them to the many fascinating "immigrant stories" that are now available for children. Especially in classrooms where there are non-native speakers of English or newly immigrated students, such books can foster understanding, acceptance, and friendship. Teacher Created Materials thematic unit *Immigration* (TCM 234), for intermediate grades, is a good source of ideas for a unit on the topic.

◆ Seek out fiction that depicts young people from more than one culture working and playing together in harmony. Such works will serve as a nice counterbalance to books that emphasize cultural diversity. Certainly, characters from all cultures should be depicted in an authentic, respectful manner as opposed to being "white-washed."

◆ Use multicultural literature to dispel stereotypes regarding people of all cultural backgrounds. Any well-written work of multicultural literature can be used for this purpose, especially if teachers promote post-reading discussions designed to emphasize the individual qualities of characters.

◆ Develop students' critical thinking skills by helping them make cross-cultural comparisons between the myths and folktales that are part of every culture. Activities of this nature will demonstrate both the intriguing differences and the amazing similarities that can be found from culture to culture. The end result will be a greater appreciation for the creativity displayed by all human beings. Teacher Created Materials thematic unit *Multicultural Folk Tales* (TCM 230) provides a model for these comparisons.

◆ Have students keep a reading log of multicultural books read. A reading passport for primary grades is provided on page 5, and a log for grades three through eight is found on page 6.

◆ Use the reproducible art found throughout the bibliography to decorate bulletin boards encouraging reading. The art may also be used as story starters, or to accompany book reviews, or as part of student art projects designed to generate interest in multicultural literature.

Title _____

Author _____

Culture _____

Picture and sentence about story:

A Trip Around

the World

Title _____

Author _____

Language(s) spoken by the characters: _____

Country and continent where the story takes place: _____

Interesting facts about life in this part of the world: _____

Read Your Way Around the World!

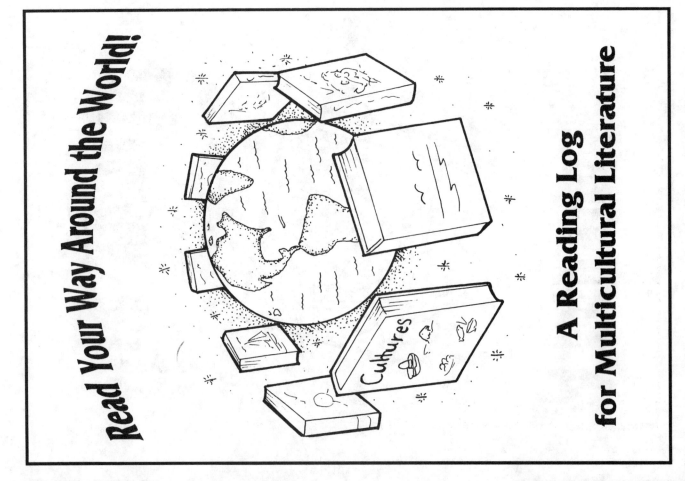

Cultures

A Reading Log
for Multicultural Literature

Preschool Through Second Grade

Aekyung's Dream. Min Paek.

See page 50 for entry.

All the Colors of the Race. Arnold Adoff. Illustrated by John Steptoe. Beech Tree Books, 1992. 56 pages. (0-688-11496-2)

Adoff has written a thought-provoking and sensitive assortment of short poems that challenges the conventional wisdom regarding race. Each poem has been written from the point of view of a young girl whose mother is an African American Protestant and father, a Caucasian Jew. Her musings and insights can enlighten primary student and adult alike. Embellished with John Steptoe's brown-hued drawings, this collection touches upon issues of vital concern to all Americans today. A brief sample should make this clear but cannot do justice to the range of themes developed in Adoff's poetry.

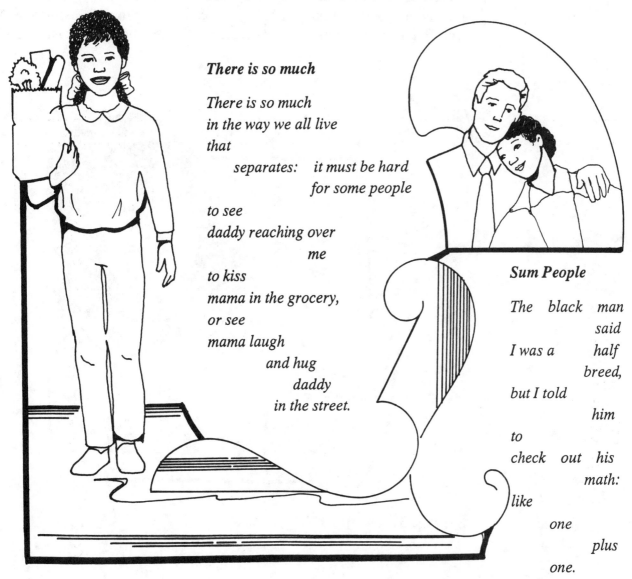

There is so much

There is so much
in the way we all live
that
        separates: it must be hard
                        for some people
to see
daddy reaching over
                        me
to kiss
mama in the grocery,
or see
mama laugh
        and hug
            daddy
            in the street.

Sum People

The   black   man
            said
I was a   half
            breed,
but I told
            him
to
check   out   his
            math:
like
    one
        plus
    one.

Amazing Grace. Mary Hoffman. Illustrated by Caroline Binch. Dial Books, 1991. 24 pages. (0-8037-1040-2)

Aladdin, Joan of Arc, Hiawatha, Anansi — Grace considers exciting characters such as these the perfect material on which to exercise her imaginative talents. Donning makeshift costumes, she spends hours playing the parts of all her favorite heroes, no matter their race or gender. So when her teacher asks for volunteers to play Peter Pan in a class production, Grace eagerly raises her hand. Immediately classmate Raj says, "You can't be Peter — that's a boy's name." Then Natalie whispers, "You can't be Peter Pan. . . . He isn't black." Despite these remarks, Grace keeps her hand up, indicating her desire to audition next week. Not until she arrives home does she finally let her hurt feelings and shaken confidence show. Both Ma and Nana notice her dejection and by way of pep-talks and a trip to see a beautiful black ballerina from Trinidad dance the role of Juliet, they help rebuild Grace's belief that she can be anything she wants to be if she puts her mind to it. Renewed self-esteem and lots of rehearsal result in the unanimous decision to have Grace play Peter. An appropriate vehicle for demonstrating to young students the importance of maintaining self-confidence and determination, this beautifully illustrated Book of the Month Club selection would be an effective starting point for a literature-based unit on goal-setting. It could also promote discussions focused on equal opportunity for people of all races and both sexes.

Angel Child, Dragon Child. Maria Michele Surat.

See page 51 for entry.

Argentina. Karen Jacobsen. Childrens Press, 1990. 48 pages. (0-516-41101-2)

See page 51 for entry.

Bá-Năm. Jeanne M. Lee. Henry Holt, 1987. 29 pages. (0-8050-0169-7)

When she first encounters the weathered, black-toothed old grave keeper Bá-Năm, Nan shrinks from her friendly overtures. However later on, while in the midst of a terrifying lightening storm, the young girl readily accepts the safety of the old woman's embrace. Though Nan is Vietnamese, frolics among monkey-filled mango trees, and places incense beside the graves of her ancestors on Thanh-Minh Day, primary students of all cultural backgrounds will certainly understand the message of this story. They will see the foolishness of Nan's having rejected a kindly person like Bá-Năm based solely on her appearance. Lee's drawings do a fine job of revealing the characters' emotions — the darkened graveyard scenes in particular effectively convey the comfort Bá-Năm offers Nan. Teachers will find this story helpful in broaching the subject of prejudice with early primary students — they can begin by talking about the characteristics found in Bá-Năm and other elderly people that might at first seem disturbing to youngsters and then progress to discussions focused on people whose unfamiliar speech, dress, or behavior might cause students to judge them unfairly.

Baby Rattlesnake. Te Ata. Adapted by Lynn Moroney. Illustrated by Veg Reisberg. Children's Book Press, 1989. 32 pages. (0-89239-049-2)

Originating with well-known Chickasaw Indian storyteller Te Ata, this simple fable will both teach and amuse young students, most of whom will surely identify with Baby Rattlesnake's desire to grow up too quickly. Impatiently yearning to enjoy adult privilege before he can accept adult responsibility, the rattleless little creature weeps and wails until a council of the Rattlesnake People agrees to give him a rattle, primarily in the hopes they will finally get little peace and quiet and a restful night's sleep. Despite the warnings of his elders, the playful baby ends up abusing his gift and finally losing it when he purposely frightens the Indian chief's daughter, who inadvertently severs the rattle from Baby's tail. The vivid colors and cartoon-like quality of Reisberg's pictures capture both the humor and Southwestern setting of this appealing book appropriate for use during a multicultural introduction to the fable.

Baby-O. Nancy White Carlstrom. Illustrated by Sucie Stevenson. Little, Brown and Co., 1992. 28 pages. (0-316-12851-1)

A catchy beat inspired by Caribbean rhythms infuses the text of this kid-pleasing book:

Chickens running in the garden patch,

Running in the morning sun.

Try and catch.

Chuka Chuka

Chuka Chuka

Sing a song of Baby-O,

Sing it soft, now, sing it slow.

Chuka Chuka

Listen to the way our baby goes,

Baby Baby Baby-O.

This same pattern is repeated again and again with varying content until each member of the "Family-O" has been honored in a verse. Youngsters will love Stevenson's colorful depictions of island life and beg to hear the book read again and again until they have it memorized. Why not get out the map and let students see just where Baby-O and his family reside?

Best-Loved Folktales of the World. Selected and with an introduction by Joanna Cole. Illustrated by Jill Karla Schwarz. Doubleday, 1982. 792 pages.
(0-385-18949-41495)

Bulging with two hundred folktales, this anthology has the potential to enrich the social studies and languages arts curricula at all levels. Drawn from cultures the world over, the tales are arranged in the following geographically based groupings: West Europe, British Isles, Scandinavia and Northern Europe, Eastern Europe, Middle East, Asia, The Pacific, Africa, North America, Caribbean and West Indies, and Central and South America. Taking advantage of this format, teachers and students can easily supplement materials found in social studies texts with literature reflecting the traditional cultures of a specific region being studied. An index that lists the tales according to category would facilitate projects involving the comparison of like-themed tales from different cultures. The categories under which the tales are listed include "Wise Men and Judges," "Talking Animals," "Fables and Tales with a Moral," "Trickster-Heroes and Clever People," "Men and Boys," and "Women and Girls." Particularly useful to teachers would be the categories "Especially Good for Young Children" and "Wonderful for Reading Aloud." Advanced students and teachers will be interested in Cole's introductory essay "Enjoying the World's Folktales," in which she discusses the role story telling has played in traditional societies and examines several theories that attempt to explain how it is that stories with similar themes or plots evolved in geographically distant cultures.

Birthday. John Steptoe.   See page 52 for entry.

Bread Bread Bread. Ann Morris. Photography by Ken Heyman. Lothrop, Lee & Shepard, 1989. 31 pages. (0-688-06334-9)

Who loves bread? Italians and Indians, Israelis and Indonesians, Ghanans, Guatemalans, and Greeks, Portuguese and Peruvians and so on and so on —in short, people the world over love it. They munch on an endless variety from the flat to the twisted to the mounded and the rounded, all of which is made abundantly clear in this beautifully photographed tribute to variety. The minimal text provides fitting accompaniment to Heyman's charming pictures of the many-hued, multicultural bakers, vendors, and consumers of this essential food stuff. The index providing basic facts about each picture and maybe a globe or large wall map are all that early primary teachers will need to employ this book as a primer for the study of world cultures.

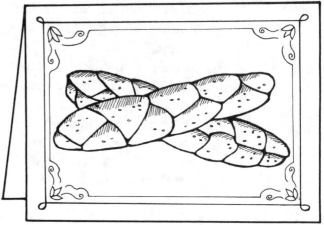

The Calypso Alphabet. John Agard. Illustrated by Jennifer Bent. Henry Holt, 1989. 27 pages. (0-8050-1177-3)

Agard, a native of Guyana, has created an alphabet book seasoned with Caribbean sights, rhythms, and lore:

> *A for Anancy.*
> *Spiderman of tricky-ticky fame.*
> *B for bat and ball.*
> *That's cricket. Play the game.*
> *C for Caribs.*
> *From them Caribbean got its name.*

A lack of familiarity with Caribbean culture should not discourage teachers from enjoying this book right along with their students; a helpful page of notes provides background information that will enable them to explain, for example, that Anancy is "a popular folk figure who by cunning almost always comes out on top" or that Caribs are "one of the Amerindian peoples who inhabited the Caribbean archipelago." Bent's vibrant illustrations, a combination of scratch-board and concentrated watercolor inks, enhance meaning as well as add visual appeal. Why not expose students to a rich cultural heritage while teaching them the alphabet? The fun they will have with this colorful book continues clear up through "Z for zombie/ A walking dead! No laughing matter" or maybe it is.

The Children of Nepal.
Reijo Harkonen.
Photography by Matti A.
Pitkanen. Carolrhoda
Books, 1990. 48 pages.
(0-87614-395-8)

Part of the series *The World's Children* which "introduces young readers to the daily life of children from different parts of the world, as well as to the history and geography of their homelands," this colorful depiction of life in Nepal has the potential to enlighten readers of all ages regarding one of the least developed countries in the world. Taking center stage, Pitkanen's splendid photographs include a culturally revealing shot of sacred cows basking in the sun before the temple at Bhaktapur and an eye-catching view of snow-covered Mt. Everest glimpsed through an emerald and ruby screen composed of bamboo and poinsettia. Especially appealing are the close up portraits of children and adults representing several of the many distinctive Nepali ethnic groups. The text, in addition to serving as captions for the photos, provides interesting bits of information that would be of particular interest to students in the intermediate grades and above, e.g., the fact that for almost one hundred years up until 1951 the reigning Ranas permitted no outsiders to enter Nepal. A map, pronunciation guide, and a table of vital statistics also help to make more familiar a not-so-distant corner of our ever-shrinking world, a place called home by nearly twenty million human beings.

Children of the Yukon.
Ted Harrison. Tundra
Books, 1991. 23 pages.
(0-88776-163-1)

Author/illustrator Ted Harrison has created an attractive piece of nonfiction that is full of richly colored paintings and interesting bits of detail regarding life in northwestern Canada's sparsely populated Yukon Territory. Harrison came to this chilly 207,076 square mile area in 1968 to teach and immediately fell in love with the place: "I turned to my wife and said: 'This is Shangri-la.' Not a very original observation perhaps, but it did express my feelings at having come across a secret world of incredible beauty and peace." Holding to this initial impression of the Yukon, he remained there as a teacher and observer, gathering the material that he has recorded in this work, which he himself describes: "What I have painted in this book are scenes that have impressed me. It is not a complete picture. Children in the towns of the Yukon do many things other North American children do. . . . But they also do things children further south never have a chance to do, and this is what I have painted." The unique activities available to children of the Yukon include walking home from school in darkness on a mid-afternoon in November, exploring the many ghost towns left from the Klondike gold strike of 1896, hunting for moose, and fishing through the ice. The children who are descendants of the native Athabascans struggle to maintain their traditional way of life by smoking moosehides, hunting caribou above the Arctic Circle, and celebrating *tauk ee tee see go* (Joyous Summer Day Festival). The youngest of students can enjoy Harrison's vibrant art work while older students will also appreciate the fascinating information presented in the text.

The Children's Jewish Holiday Kitchen. Joan
Nathan. Schocken Books,
1987. 127 pages.
(0-8052-0827-5)

As teachers know, the preparation and consumption of ethnic foods is a pleasurable means of developing students' cultural awareness. Here is a cookbook tailor-made for combining lessons in cooking and culture. The book is divided into chapters, one for each of ten important Jewish holidays — Sabbath, Rosh Hashanah, Yom Kippur, Sukkot, Hanukkah, Tu B'Shevat, Purim, Passover, Israeli Independence Day, and Shavuot. Chapters begin with a discussion of the holidays' historical backgrounds, customs involved in their celebration, foods traditionally prepared for the celebrations, and suggested menus. The recipes themselves have been modified in some cases so that children can successfully participate in their preparation. Also of interest is a prefatory chapter that explains the origins and rules of *kosher* cooking. Here is a sample menu for the celebration of Passover:

CHILD-CENTERED SEDER MENU
Chicken Soup with Matzah Balls
Turkey
Vegetable and Fruit Kugel Cupcakes
Baby Moses Salad
Fresh Strawberries
Chocolate-chip Kisses

The Chinese Mirror.
Mirra Ginsburg. Illustrated
by Margot Zemach.
Harcourt Brace
Javanovich, 1988. 27
pages. (0-15-200420-3)

This adaptation of a Korean folktale takes place "long, long ago" in a village whose residents have never seen a mirror until the day a traveller brings one of these intriguing, shiny objects back home from China. None of the unsophisticated villagers who curiously sneak a peak into the strange reflective disk is able to determine the identity of the face staring back at him. Much argument and bewilderment results until an irate man, accusing his own image of being a big fat bully, retaliates by shattering the mirror and puts an end to all the confusion. Inspired by the paintings of two eighteenth-century Korean genre painters Sin Yun-bok and Kim Hong-do, Zemach's watercolor illustrations emphasize the antic behavior of adults and children alike. Students will find this tale amusing as they ponder the naivety of the villagers and may be inspired to write their own humorous stories describing the behavior they imagine people might have displayed "long, long ago" when they first encountered various other simple objects such as the wheel, a shoe, or a toothbrush.

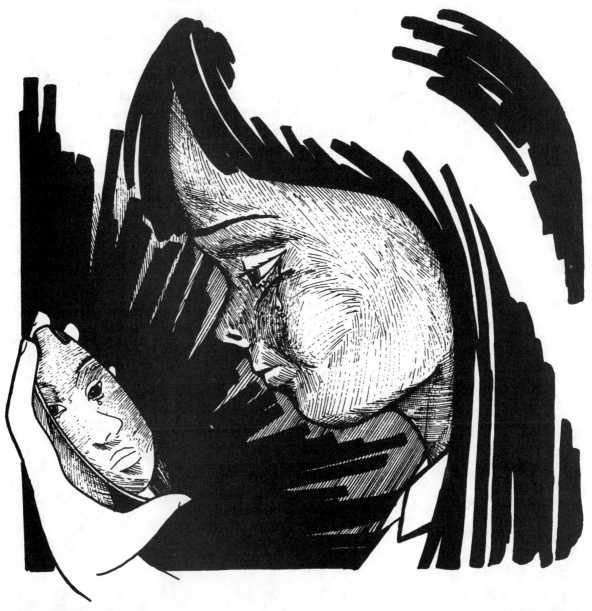

Cleversticks. Bernard Ashley. Illustrated by Derek Brazell. Crown Publishers, 1991. 29 pages. (0-517-58878-1)

Ling Sung, an early primary student in a multiracial class, decides after only two days that he has had enough of going to school. The problem has nothing to do with the fact that he is Asian American — he's just one of those kids who hasn't yet found his forte. He can't tie his shoes, the way Terry can or write his name, the way Manjit can. He can't even button up his jacket quite right, the way Sharon can, and he is fed up with watching all the other students demonstrate their abilities and get heaps of praise from their fellow classmates and from Ms. Smith and Ms. Dhanjal, the two teachers. Finally on the third day of school, Ling Sung has his moment of glory. When he accidently breaks his cookie into several pieces, he decides to use two wooden paintbrushes like chopsticks to put the pieces of cookie in his mouth. Suddenly, everybody — including the teachers — wants Ling Sung to demonstrate how to eat with chopsticks. He does just that, and in return for his help, Terry, Manjit, and Sharon teach him their special skills. After school when Ling Sung excitedly tells his dad about his great day, his dad pronounces him "a real cleversticks!" This story authentically recreates a situation encountered by many students when they first enter school. Teachers will find this book an excellent vehicle for beginning discussions on self-esteem. They can explain how important it is for students to recognize and praise each other's accomplishments. In addition, they can point out that students of various cultural backgrounds have special knowledge to share with their classmates. Emphasizing the rewards of attending a multicultural school are Brazell's appealing drawings depicting a harmonious classroom atmosphere in which students of various ethnicities interact warmly.

Count Your Way through the Arab World. Jim Haskins.

See page 55 for entry.

Count Your Way through China. Jim Haskins.

See page 55 for entry.

Count Your Way through Japan. Jim Haskins.

See page 56 for entry.

Count Your Way through Mexico. Jim Haskins.

See page 56 for entry.

A Country Far Away. Nigel Gray. Illustrated by Philippe Dupasquier. Orchard, 1988. 26 pages. (0-531-07024-7)

A picture book that's truly worth a thousand words, this comparison between the lives of two children — a white boy in a European or North American suburban setting and a black boy in what appears to be a coastal African village — portrays the basic human experiences shared by those living in cultures that, geographically, are worlds apart. A single first-person narrative that speaks for both boys introduces each set of colorful illustrations detailing activities that include helping mom and dad, finishing off the last day of the school year, celebrating the birth of a baby sister, and contemplating a map of our world filled with many potential new friends living in far away places. Even the youngest of students will gain wonderful insight into human differences *and* similarities by reading the very simple text and poring over the pictures that bring it to life. One of *Parent's Magazine's* Best Books of the Year and a NCSS-CBC Notable Children's Trade Book in the Field of Social Studies, this work belongs on the bookshelf of every primary classroom.

A Crocodile's Tale: A Philippine Folk Story. Jose and Ariane Aruego. Scholastic, 1976. 32 pages. (0-590-09899-3)

The Aruegos have created a winsome group of drawings to accompany this folklore-based fable that begins when little Jaun is walking near the river and hears someone crying. Looking up through the lush Philippine jungle growth, he spies a large green crocodile tied to a tree. Empathy motivates him to rescue the creature, but he soon finds that the crocodile intends to reward his efforts by carrying him into river and eating him up. Stunned by the injustice of it all, Jaun cries, "That isn't fair! . . . You can't eat me. I just saved your life." Devoid of all gratitude, the crocodile is about begin his meal when Juan convinces the brute to let him consult an old basket and hat, which are floating down the river. Much to Juan's chagrin, each recommends that the crocodile go ahead and eat the boy — after all, in their experience humans show no gratitude so why should a crocodile? Finally a clever, sympathetic monkey lures the crocodile close enough to shore that Juan can jump to safety. Proclaiming that he will always be grateful, Juan acts upon the monkey's request that he persuade his father to plant more bananas and look the other way when the monkey is feasting upon the fruit. Juan's appropriate show of appreciation brings good feelings to both himself and the monkey. Primary students will enjoy the drawings of Juan and the animals and be well-prepared for a discussion about the merits of gratitude.

Crow Boy. Taro Yashima. Puffin, 1976. 34 pages. (0-14-050172-X)

Pain brought about as a result of intracultural intolerance is central to the story of Chibi, an undersized Japanese boy whose unconventional behavior brings him ridicule and isolation during all but the last of his six years at the village school. Taking refuge in his own world where the wild grapes and the raucous crows become his companions, Chibi develops abilities that go unnoticed until Mr. Isobe, the kindly new teacher, takes an interest in them. When Mr. Isobe announces at the talent show that Chibi will perform crow voice imitations, no one is prepared to witness the amazing ability he has acquired through years of diligent observation and practice. Tears of remorse fill the eyes of those who had once called Chibi stupid, and soon he is renamed Crow Boy in honor of his newly recognized skill and status. Colorful pictures and an easy-to-follow story line make this Caldecott Honor Book a winner for primary teachers striving to help students appreciate the need to look for the worth in all people, no matter how unlike ourselves they may seem.

The Day of Ahmed's Secret. Florence Parry Heide and Judith Heide Gilliland. Illustrated by Ted Lewin. Lothrop, Lee, & Shepard, 1990. 30 pages. (0-688-08894-5)

The daily life of young Ahmed as he delivers his load of fuel along the streets of modern-day Cairo is revealed by way of an informative first-person narrative and wonderful, detailed watercolors. American students will get a taste of the rich variety of sights, sounds, occupations, architecture, and modes of transportation that fill a world that may seem quite different from their own. Though they may be surprised by exotic phenomena such as Cairo's rosewater vendors, camel caravans, donkey carts, robed and shawled citizens, and surrounding desert and pyramids, they will also discover they have much in common with the Arab protagonist, in particular, a great pride in learning to write. All day long as Ahmed travels about the city, he is reveling in the knowledge that he will be able to surprise his family with his newly acquired skill. When he arrives home that night, he proudly demonstrates over and over again his ability to form his name in Arabic script, thinking to himself that his name now may last "longer than the sound of it, maybe even lasting, like the old buildings in the city, a thousand years." Discussion of both text and pictures will acquaint students with an important corner of the Arab world and humanize its inhabitants.

Diego. Jonah Winter. See page 58 for entry.

Down Under: Vanishing Cultures. Jan Reynolds. See page 58 for entry.

The Egyptian Cinderella. Shirley Climo. See page 59 for entry.

Elinda Who Danced in the Sky: An Estonian Folktale. Adapted by Lynn Moroney. See page 60 for entry.

An Ellis Island Christmas.
Maxinne Rhea Leighton.
Illustrated by Dennis
Nolan. Viking, 1992. 32
pages. (0-670-83182-4)

With the story of her own father's journey from Poland to America in mind, the author has written a fictional narrative in which Krysia Petrowski describes what it was like, at the age of six, to make this same journey. When Krysia's mother first announces her intent to leave for America where "tables are filled with food, and there are no soldiers with guns in the street," Krysia feels mixed emotions; though plenty of food and no soldiers sound "like a fairy tale," she does not want to leave behind her home or her friend Michi. But she has no time to agonize over the situation because that very night she finds herself packing and in the morning is off, walking for many days to reach the sea. She recounts the events of her difficult ocean voyage in vivid terms that young students can appreciate, as is demonstrated in this passage describing the tenth day: "Everyone was throwing up. It was disgusting. It smelled so bad. The water was getting rougher. One afternoon, the sky got black and thick like mud. The ocean got fatter. The waves grew taller and taller as the boat rocked from side to side. Water began to flood the deck." Krysia's account of catching her first glimpse of the Statue of Liberty and disembarking at Ellis Island on Christmas Eve is equally full of descriptive detail that will help primary students understand the excitement and apprehension that filled the hearts of immigrants as they worked their way through the bureaucratic maze in hopes of gaining entry to the mainland. Nolan's evocative illustrations play a major role in bringing Krysia's story to life.

Everett Anderson's Goodbye. Lucille Clifton. Illustrated by Ann Grifalconi. Henry Holt, 1983. 20 pages. (0-8050-0235-9)

After making many painful adjustments following the death of his father, little Everett Anderson is finally able to say, "I knew/ my daddy loved me through and through,/and whatever happens when people die,/love doesn't stop, and/neither will I." These closing lines of Clifton's sensitive poem reflect a peace of mind and will to survive that were hard won. They come about only after Everett has passed through all the five stages of grief: denial, anger, bargaining, depression, and acceptance. As testament to the skill with which this book was created, the essence of each of these stages is poignantly communicated with a few simple words and less than a dozen soft black and white drawings. Young readers who have suffered the loss of a loved one will find comfort and hope in this beautifully illustrated Reading Rainbow Book and winner of the Coretta Scott King Award. Primary teachers and school counselors might want to have several copies on hand to loan to the parents of grieving students. The fact that Everett is African American may make this book especially appropriate for black students, but students of all colors could certainly find consolation in its message.

Everybody Cooks Rice.
Norah Dooley. Illustrated
by Peter J. Thornton.
Carolrhoda Books, 1991.
27 pages. (0-87614-412-1)

Life in an integrated community can be not only interesting but also downright delicious as Carrie learns one afternoon when she visits the homes of her neighbors, looking for her brother Anthony. Anthony, who already realizes the delights of multicultural cookery, makes a habit of wandering from house to house to sample the potpourri of neighborhood cuisines. On this particular afternoon, it happens that everybody is cooking an ethnic rice dish, so Carrie soon discovers the variety of flavors produced when particular ingredients and cooking techniques are used in preparing this popular grain. By the time Carrie arrives home, she is stuffed, having tasted recipes which originate from six countries — Barbados, Puerto Rico, Vietnam, India, China, and Haiti — and is too full to eat any of her mom's luscious *risi e bisi*, a northern Italian dish passed down from Carrie's great grandmother. Students can enjoy preparing each of the simple rice dishes mentioned in the story by following the recipes provided at the end of this attractive book. Thorton's bright illustrations highlight the neighborly hospitality with which Carrie is greeted as she enters each kitchen and, in combination with the text, clearly demonstrate the joys of living in a multicultural society.

Eyes of the Dragon.
Margaret Leaf.

See page 62 for entry.

A Family in Japan. Judith Elkin.

See page 62 for entry.

Favorite Tales from Many Lands. Walter Retan. Illustrated by Linda Medley. Grosset & Dunlap, 1989. (0-448-19183-0)

Retan has skillfully retold the tales comprising this attractive collection in a fast-paced, easy-to-understand style that will engross the youngest audiences. For older students, the lessons embedded in each story will provide ample food for thought, discussion, and writing assignments. Colorful illustrations emphasize the multicultural origins of the following fourteen tales gathered here, some of which are very familiar while most are less so: Norway's "The Three Billy Goats Gruff," Spain's "Little Half-Chick," India's "Tit for Tat," Germany's "The Wolf and the Seven Little Kids," Russia's "The Little Snow Maiden," Rumania's "Why the Woodpecker Has a Long Beak," Japan's "Little Peachling," England's "Lazy Jack," France's "The Three Wishes," Central Africa's "Why the Cat and Rat Are No Longer Friends," the Delaware Tribe's "The Eagles of Lost Opportunity," Mexico's "The Boy Who Made a Snake," China's "The Wonderful Pear Tree," and West Africa's "How There Came to Be Anansi Stories." These tales will certainly demonstrate to students that imaginative excitement and humor are gifts bestowed upon the world by many different cultures.

Family Pictures/Cuadros de familia. Carmen Lomas Garza. Transcribed by Harriet Rohmer. Translated by Rosalma Zubizarreta. Children's Book Press, 1990. 32 pages. (0-89239-050-6)

Accomplished Mexican-American painter Carmen Lomas Garza presents in detailed, jewel-toned paintings events from her life as a child growing up in Kingsville, Texas. Each painting is accompanied by a description, written in both Spanish and English, that Garza provided during interviews with editor Harriet Rohmer. Most of the events depicted involve family activities: harvesting grandparents' oranges, preparing tamales, celebrating Garza's sixth birthday, swimming off Padre Island, sitting on the porch eating watermelon on a hot summer night. In addition to these are scenes that provide information about the Hispanic community at large, for example, a cakewalk held to raise money for sending Mexican Americans to the university, a curandera using folk remedies to treat an ill neighbor, and the reenactment of the Christmas story during Las Posadas. The final painting shows Garza and her sister gazing up at a full moon from the rooftop of their house as they dream of the future. In the accompanying text, Garza discusses the outcome of her plans: "I knew since I was 13 years old that I wanted to be an artist. And all those things that I dreamed of doing as an artist, I'm finally doing now. My mother was the one who inspired me . . . ." Garza's attractive pictorial autobiography will likewise inspire students to pursue their own dreams, as well as contribute to their understanding of Hispanic American culture.

Fiesta! Cinco de Mayo.
June Behrens.
Photography by Scott
Taylor. Childrens Press,
1978. 32 pages.
(0-516-48815-5)

The special appeal of this book lies in its multicultural approach to the exploration of Cinco de Mayo; not only do Taylor's colorful photographs depict children of various races enjoying the festivities but Behrens clearly explains the significance this holiday holds for all North Americans: "The fifth of May is a joyous festival day, a very special day for Mexican Americans. It is an important day for all the people in American. On May 5, 1862, there was a big battle in the town of Puebla, Mexico. In a battle with the French army the poor, ragged Mexican army won a great victory. The victory helped to drive foreigners out of North America. No foreign power has invaded North America since." If this is not enough to capture the attention of young readers, the allure of Cinco de Mayo's Mariachi bands, delicious tortilla-based dishes, songs and dances, and piñata parties certainly will; these are all amply described in Behren's easy-to-read prose and vividly portrayed in the many photos accompanying it. Primary students would find this a highly accessible book for the independent reading that might be involved with a cross-cultural study of holidays.

Follow the Drinking Gourd. Jeanette Winter.

See page 64 for entry.

The Fool and the Fish: A Tale from Russia. Alexander Nikolayevich Afanasyev.

See page 64 for entry.

Friday Night Is Papa Night. Ruth A. Sonneborn. Illustrated by Emily A. McCully. Puffin, 1987. 26 pages. (0-14-050754-X)

Though lacking details of setting and culture that would help identify the specific nationality and ethnicity of its characters (only a cover blurb from the *Kirkus Review* specifies a "Puerto Rican milieu"), this rather generic Hispanic story is nevertheless appealing and lifelike. Little Pedro, sitting on his bed in the kitchen watching Mama mop the floor, asks sadly: "Why doesn't Papa come home every night? Ana's papa comes home every night. Why not my papa?" Mama explains that Papa must work at two distant jobs to provide food and shelter for Pedro, Manuela, Carlos, Ricardo, Mama, and himself. Pedro is heartened when he remembers that "tonight is Friday night," the night Papa is finally able to come home each week. The story continues with the excitement of preparing for Papa's homecoming, the disappointment everyone feels when Papa fails to return on time, and the relief and joy all experience when he finally comes in the middle of the night after having been delayed by an ill friend. Illustrated with warm yellow and brown drawings depicting the domestic life of a close-knit Hispanic family, this book would make a worthwhile addition to any primary classroom where there are students who would benefit from an easy-to-read story about a hardworking, loving family.

Games of the World: How to Make Them, How to Play Them, How They Came to Be, special English edition for the National Committees for UNICEF in Australia, Canada, Ireland, and Switzerland. Frederic V. Grunfeld. Swiss Committee for UNICEF, 1982. 280 pages.

A resource that teachers will refer to time and again to get ideas for art projects, physical education activities, and social studies units, this book will also fascinate young students with its many colorful photographs of modern-day gamesters and art works depicting ancient revelry. In addition, older students will enjoy reading the detailed information that accompanies every one of the entries for the more than one hundred games discussed. Each entry includes a history of a particular game, detailed directions for playing the game, and explicit directions for making all required equipment. The games are arranged in five categories — board and table games; street and playground games; field and forest games; party and festival games; and puzzles, tricks, and stunts. The potential this book has for promoting multiculturalism is indicated in the forward written by Eduard Spescha of the Swiss Committee for UNICEF: "These pages are filled with ideas, information, instruction and suggestions from all corners of the world. They show us that games know no boundaries, that when it comes to play — to this basic expression of human life — there is only one world. In extending our possibilities for play and in deepening our understanding for the different games, we come to realise that we depend on one another for our development."

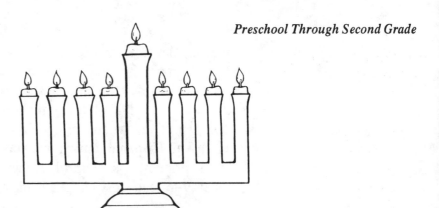

Hanukkah! Roni Schotter. Illustrated by Marylin Hafner. Little, Brown and Co., 1990. 29 pages. (0-316-77466-9)

An affectionate family of eight share the traditions of Hanukkah in this delightful melding of Schotter's vivacious text and Hafner's adorable illustrations. Three generations consisting of Grandma Rose; Mama and Papa; and Nora, Dan, Ruthie, Sam, and Baby Moe join together to light the menorah, sing a song of prayer, play dreydel, exchange gifts, and prepare and enjoy a delicious meal. Even Baby Moe, whose amusing attempts to say Hanukkah will tickle young readers, gets right in on all the action: " 'Yes, dreydel,' Sam says. 'For Hanukkah. Say Hanukkah, Moe.' 'Anoohanh, Moe,' Moe says. 'Anoohah!' and drools on Sam's foot." Following the story are a short essay containing information about the historical origins of Hanukkah and a brief glossary defining "dreydel," "latkes," "menorah," and "shamash." With the aid of the essay and glossary, teachers unfamiliar with Hanukkah will be prepared to answer students' questions.

Hawaii Is a Rainbow. Stephanie Feeney. Photography by Jeff Reese. University of Hawaii Press, 1985. 61 pages. (0-8248-1007-4)

A dazzling picture book that is more than just a picture book, this work consists of two parts — the first contains a collection of brilliantly colorful uncaptioned photographs spotlighting Hawaiian people, places, plants, and animals; the second consists of separate articles on Hawaiian geography, biology, and history as well as several pages of small photos described in detailed captions. The first section introduces young children to the colors of the rainbow, its pictures grouped in bunches according to their dominant colors, with orange-hued photos following the red, yellow following orange, and so forth. In addition to teaching about color, the first section provides preschoolers as well as older students with visual proof of Hawaii's breath-taking diversity: "Hawaii is, in some ways, like a rainbow. Many different colors are seen on the islands and they seem more vivid in the clear air and bright sunshine. . . . The people of Hawaii are also like the rainbow. They come from many places in the world, have skin, hair, and eyes of different colors, speak many languages, and have different kinds of food, celebrations, and art. Like the colors of the rainbow when people come together they seem even more beautiful." The informative written text found in the introduction and the second section can be read to younger students while older students can enjoy it as independent readers. Whichever is the case, this lovely book will provide students of all ages with a view of multiculturalism at its beautiful best.

Himalaya: Vanishing Cultures. Jan Reynolds.

See page 66 for entry.

Hoang Anh: A Vietnamese-American Boy. Diane Hoyt-Goldsmith.

See page 67 for entry.

Hopscotch Around the World. Mary D. Lankford.

See page 68 for entry.

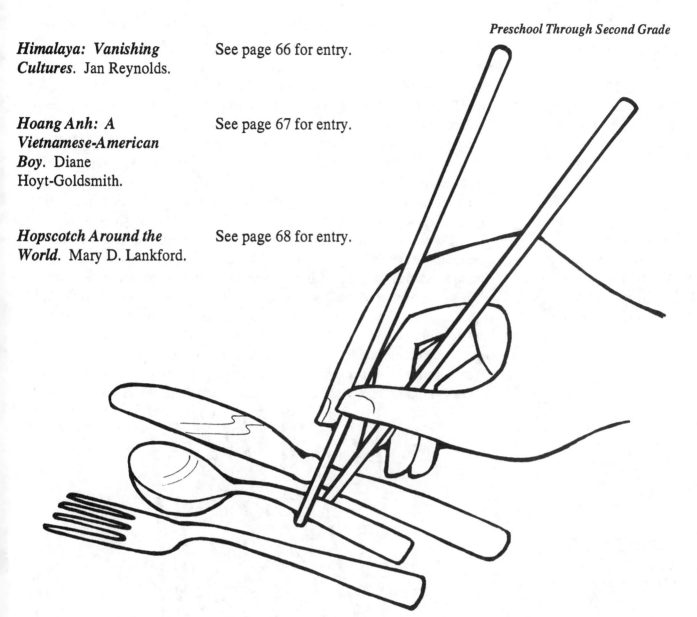

How My Parents Learned to Eat. Ina R. Friedman. Illustrated by Allen Say. Houghton Mifflin, 1984. 32 pages. (0-395-44235-4)

As described by their young daughter, the courtship of John, an American sailor stationed in Yokohama, and Aiko, a Japanese student, was a sweet and humorous affair filled with long walks and long talks but no shared meals. Afraid to ask Aiko to dinner because he had never eaten with chopsticks, John wondered how he would ever be able to propose marriage. As for Aiko, she fretted over the supposition that John had never invited her to dinner because of her ineptitude with a knife and fork. Finally, each summoned the courage to learn the other's customs, which eventually resulted in the establishment of a happy household where both chopsticks and Western-style utensils are regularly used. A Reading Rainbow Selection illustrated with Allen Say's lovely watercolors, this book will not only amuse students but also teach them an important lesson: the meeting of different cultures can produce wonderful results if efforts are made to overcome initial awkwardness and embarrassment. A unit on multicultural cooking and eating practices could be built around Friedman's charming story as could discussions of bicultural families.

I Speak English for My Mom. Muriel Stanek. Illustrated by Judith Friedman. Albert Whitman, 1989. 29 pages. (0-8075-3659-8)

Lupe Gómez understands that her Mexican American mother could not survive life in Chicago without her aid, given the fact that Lupe translates at the medical clinic, on shopping excursions, at student-teacher conferences, and during mail reading/bill paying sessions. Although Lupe makes it clear that she enjoys helping out, she also admits, "Sometimes, I don't want to speak for my mother. I'd rather be with my friends." When the widowed Mrs. Gómez learns she may lose her job at a garment factory, she assures Lupe all will be well. But both mother and daughter realize that job opportunities are limited by the inability to speak English. A flyer posted on a bulletin board at the laundromat prompts Mrs. Gómez to overcome some initial jitters and enroll in free English classes. Before long, Lupe is helping her mother with homework, and they are carrying on simple conversations in English; however, they soon revert to Spanish. This portrayal of a situation experienced by millions will seem realistic to students with non-English-speaking parents — no matter what their nationality — and certainly will let them know they are not alone in feeling some ambivalence about their parents' dependence upon them. Lovely black and white pencil drawings accompany a text that contains a bit of Spanish dialogue, which Lupe always restates in English.

The Inch Boy. Junko Morimoto. Puffin, 1988. 29 pages. (0-14-050677-2)

Having prayed to the Buddah week after week in hopes of achieving parenthood, a gentle old Japanese couple suddenly find themselves blessed with a tiny child they name Issunboshi, meaning "little inch boy." As the years go by, Issunboshi grows no taller but nevertheless possesses the ambition and daring of a giant. Self-confident and proud, he travels to Kyoto in a rice bowl propelled with one of his mother's chopsticks and presents himself to Lord Sanjo as worthy of being his Samurai. Sanjo accepts Issunboshi's offer to serve him, and before the day is out, the pint-sized Samurai has saved the Princess Makiko from the clutches of the huge Red Demon, using nothing but his cunning and a sewing needle sword. Touching the demon's magic hammer transforms Issunboshi into the full-sized Samurai General Horikawa who marries the princess and gains fame throughout Japan for his courage. Morimoto's bold, colorful illustrations add much to the charm of this entertaining Japanese legend which could contribute to a study of the characteristics common to legendary heros from a variety of cultures.

The Incredible Painting of Felix Clousseau. Jon Agee. Farrar, Straus & Giroux, 1988. 29 pages. (0-374-43582-0)

The Paris art world is outraged when a short, funny-looking unknown has the temerity to enter his painting of a duck in the Royal Palace Grand Contest of Art. He has put himself in competition with the greats Gaston du Stoganoff and his "The King on His Throne," Felicien Caffayollay and his "The King on Horseback," and Alphonse LeCamembair and his "The King in Armor." Unlike his fellow artists, Clousseau has dared to break from tradition, and the judges pronounce his painting ridiculous. But before Clousseau is laughed right out of town, a loud "quack" is heard, and the duck of his creation has left its frame and is wandering around the palace. Immediately the judges change their tune, call Clousseau a genius, and award him the Grand Prize because "it was the first time in history a painting had quacked." Unfortunately, Clousseau's genius proves a bit much when volcanoes, boa constrictors, canons, and other objects in his paintings take to erupting, slithering, exploding, and so forth. Clousseaux is jailed and his paintings are confiscated. This funny, off-beat tale comes to an end when, thanks to a painting of a dog that escaped confiscation, the king's crown is saved from thieves. Clousseau is released and awarded the Medal of Honor. Both students and teachers will be tickled by Agee's words and illustrations. This book has been designated An American Library Association Notable Book, A New York Times Book Review Notable Book of the Year, A New York Times Outstanding Book of the Year, and a Fanfare on The Horn Book's Honor List.

Is Anybody Up? Ellen
Kandoian. Putnam's,
1989. 27 pages.
(0-399-21749-5)

Little Molly sometimes gets up early and goes downstairs to pour herself
some cereal. Sitting alone at the kitchen table with just her teddy bear and
a bunch of bananas to keep her company, she may feel as if she is the only
one in the whole wide world who is awake. But how wrong she is! "Far
to the north and far to the south, it is seven-thirty in the morning and other
people are getting up and having breakfast too." While Molly is crunching
on her cereal, an Inuit woman living on Baffin Bay prepares griddle cakes
and tea, a boy in Quebec fixes French toast, a kitty in New York slurps a
dish of milk, a girl in Haiti enjoys peanut butter with bananas, and so forth,
clear on down to Chile and then to the Arctic where a sailor and a seal are
breakfasting on fish. These are just some of the scenes Kandoian describes
to demonstrate what a busy and varied place the Western Hemisphere really
is. The author further emphasizes cultural variation by indicating how the
person in each scene would say "good morning" in his or her native tongue.
Using just a globe and this simple but clever book, teachers can open the
eyes of primary students to the awesome fact that the world is filled with
people who are in many ways so very much like themselves yet in other
ways, excitingly different. Kandoian's cheery watercolors, infused with
the golden glow of morning, will charm young readers. For teachers, a
short essay following the main text will help with introducing the concept
of time zones and explaining why all the different people who live in
Molly's zone — the Eastern Time Zone — set their clocks to read the same
hour.

***Kanu of Kathmandu: A
Journey in Nepal.***
Barbara A. Margolies.

See page 70 for entry.

Keepers of the Earth: Native American Stories and Environmental Activities for Children. Michael J. Caduto and Joseph Bruchac. Illustrated by John Kahionhes Fadden and Carol Wood. Fulcrum, 1988. 209 pages. (1-55591-027-0)

Teachers will find this an outstanding source of interdisciplinary lessons integrating the language arts, social studies, and science in a creative manner. Part I, brief but helpful, offers background and suggestions for using Part II, the bulk of the book. Part II consists of thematic units covering topics such as creation; fire; earth; wind and weather; water; sky; seasons; plants and animals; life, death, spirit; and unity of the earth. Within each unit are chapters, each beginning with a Native American legend pertaining to the unit topic. Following the legend are science facts and a variety of activities. The following example will help illustrate the specific format of each chapter. In the unit on plants and animals is a chapter that begins with the Anishinabe legend "Manabozho and the Maple Trees." According to this legend, Manabozho's tribe is relying too heavily on one natural resource, the maple trees. Manabozho dilutes the syrup in all the trees so that his people will have to use other means besides harvesting the syrup to supply themselves with food. Following this legend are several pages of information on sugar maples, the structure of trees, and plant succession. Next are various questions that will help students relate these science facts to the content of the legend. Then, two science activities are thoroughly explained: 1) studying the structure of trees by building models and looking at cross sections of actual tress 2) studying plant succession by building models or making field observations. Suggestions for extending these experiences include creating a poem or mural, reading about the way Native Americans used wood, and building a sensory-awareness blindfold walk.

Kenju's Forest. Junko Morimoto.

See page 70 for entry.

Klara's New World. Jeanette Winter.

See page 71 for entry.

Korea. Karen Jacobsen.

See page 71 for entry.

Kwanzaa. A. P. Porter.

See page 72 for entry.

The Legend of the Bluebonnet: An Old Tale of Texas. Retold and illustrated by Tomie dePaola. Putnam's, 1983. 28 pages. (0-399-20937-9)

She-Who-Is-Alone, the young heroine of this Comanche legend, has known great personal loss; a prolonged drought-induced famine took the lives of both her parents, and now the only tangible connection she has with her past is the beloved warrior doll made by her mother and decked with blue jay feathers supplied by her father. But dear as this doll is to her, She-Who-Is-Alone is willing to give it up to save her people. When the shaman reports that the Great Spirits demand a precious burnt offering as atonement for the Comanches' exploitation of the Earth, the selfless young girl knows precisely what she must do. After all her people have retired to their tepees, She-Who-Is-Alone carries her doll and a burning stick to the hill where the shaman communed with the spirits: "Stars filled the sky, but there was no moon. 'O great Spirits,' She-Who Is-Alone said, 'here is my warrior doll. It is the only thing I have from my family who died in this famine. It is my most valued possession. Please accept it.'" After the doll has been reduced to ashes, the girl scatters them to the wind and then collapses on the spot into a deep sleep. She awakens to find the once-parched countryside covered with lovely bluebonnet flowers, the color of jaybird feathers. Soon the rain begins to fall. The Comanches interpret the flowers and the rain as proof that the gods have been appeased, "and every spring the Great Spirits remember the sacrifice of a little girl and fill the hills and valleys of the land, now called Texas, with the beautiful blue flowers." DePaola's art work and skillful retelling of this moving tale will be enjoyed by readers of all ages.

Lion Dancer: Ernie Wan's Chinese New Year. Kate Waters and Madeline Slovenz-Low. Photography by Martha Cooper. Scholastic, 1990. 30 pages. (0-590-43047-5)

Set in New York City's Chinatown, this nonfictional work describes the Wan family's Chinese New Year celebration. Told from Ernie Wan's point-of-view, text and photos first provide some general facts about Ernie's life — he lives in an apartment with his family of five, walks the Chinatown streets appreciating the varied sights, attends public school during the week and Chinese school on the weekends, and since the age of three has been studying martial arts at his dad's kung fu school. We then learn of the careful practice required in preparing for the Lion Dance Ernie

32

will perform before the crowds on New Years Day, a performance meant to scare away evil spirits and bring good luck and honor to his family. A delicious-looking holiday feast, offerings of food and incense at the ancestral altar, firecrackers, little red money envelopes, and of course the Lion Dance itself are all colorfully portrayed in Cooper's photographs. The book concludes with a little information on the Chinese lunar calendar and horoscope. Students will be intrigued by pictures of the brilliant lion costume and will have fun comparing the traditions of Chinese New Year with those belonging to holidays celebrated in various other cultures.

Lon Po Po: A Red-Riding Hood Story from China. Ed Young.	See page 74 for entry.
Mary McLean and the St. Patrick's Day Parade. Steven Kroll.	See page 75 for entry.
Mary of Mile 18. Ann Blades.	See page 76 for entry.

Minnie's Yom Kippur Birthday. Marilyn Singer. Illustrated by Ruth Rosner. Harper & Row, 1989. 32 pages. (0-06-025846-2)

When Minnie learns that her fifth birthday falls on Yom Kippur, she wonders what will become of the traditional party, cake, and gifts. Not quite sure what is meant by "day of atonement," she can only speculate about what will happen based on her dad's brief explanation. He tells her that because Yom Kippur is the "most serious Jewish holiday of all," her birthday celebration will be different this year but wonderful in its own way. Though initially disappointed by the holiday fasting and solemnity, in the end Minnie is quite satisfied with the way her birthday turns out. Yom Kippur provides her with her first visit to the Temple, encouragement to apologize to her brother and sister (her form of atonement), and a culminating feast that is topped off with a huge fudge birthday cake shared with everyone at the Temple. Told in Minnie's own words, this story offers an entertaining introduction not only to the observance of Yom Kippur but to Temple practices in general. Minnie describes her first impressions of the ark containing the Torah, a ram's horn shofar, the cantor singing in Hebrew, and the rabbi telling the story of Jonah. Rosner's gentle-looking illustrations contribute information important to understanding a story that primary teachers will find helpful when undertaking a multicultural study of holidays or religious customs.

Molly's Pilgrim. Barbara Cohen. Illustrated by Michael J. Deraney. Bantam, 1990. 41 pages. (0-553-15833-3)

Third-grader Molly, a turn-of-the-century Russian Jewish emigré, begins her first-person narrative with a poignant simplicity that is sure to grab the attention of primary students — "I didn't like the school in Winter Hill. In Winter Hill they laughed at me" — and then continues with a story that is, at the same time, personal and culturally specific yet timeless and universal in its description of an outsider's struggle to survive in a mainstream culture where insensitive ignorance abounds. In the end it is the unabashed display of her cultural heritage that enables Molly's mother to silence Molly's tormenters. When she assists with a Thanksgiving homework assignment, instead of fashioning a traditional Anglo-looking Pilgrim doll dressed in black and white, the mother makes a beautiful likeness of herself as she appeared as a girl in Russia. The doll and Molly both gain the admiration of the students once Molly's teacher has praised the doll, explained to the children the actual meaning of "pilgrim," and pointed out the Jewish contribution to the origin of Thanksgiving. Michael Deraney's detailed black and white drawings skillfully portray the range of emotions experienced by the characters. Both illustrations and text could stimulate activities focused on the immigrant experience, foreign accents and appearance, the acceptance of human diversity, cultural pride, Jewish history and culture, and the true spirit of Thanksgiving. The movie version of *Molly's Pilgrim* won the Academy Award for Best Short Film of 1985.

Mother Goose on the Rio Grande. Francis Alexander. Illustrated by Charlotte Baker. NTC Publishing Group, 1988. 89 pages. (0-8442-7641-3)

Language learning will seem like a lively game with this bilingual book. Written in both Spanish and English, it consists of dozens of nursery rhymes, nonsense rhymes, nature rhymes, simple riddles, and verses to accompany physical play, all of which combine the "language and culture found in Mexico and the American Southwest." Neither students nor teachers will be able to resist bouncing and clapping, smiling and giggling when the classroom is filled with the likes of

Ramón sallies
Through the alleys
With a chick.
Catch him quick!

Ahí viene Ramón
por un callejón,
con una gallina.
¡Ta-rón, ta-rón!

Long as never,
pounded ever.
What is it?
(The road)

Largo, largo,
y muy amartillado
¿Qué es?
(El camino)

Mrs. Katz and Tush.
Patricia Polacco. Bantam,
1992. 30 pages.
(0-553-08122-5)

A tailless kitten — the runt of the litter that no one else wants — brings together elderly Jewish widow Mrs. Katz and Larnel, her young African American neighbor. The love they develop for Tush the cat forms a bond between them that is intensified by commonalities they discover in their cultural heritage. One day over some freshly baked kugel, Mrs. Katz mentions that after she emigrated from Poland and married Myron, they often vacationed in the Catskills at a "borscht resort, you know, a place for Jews to stay." This spurs Larnel to reveal the fact that his grandma, as an African American, had likewise been barred from staying at certain places. Mrs. Katz is then prompted to say, "Larnel, your people and mine are alike, you know. Trouble, we've seen. Happiness, too. Great strength we've had. You and I are alike, so much alike!" Soon Larnel is accompanying Mrs. Katz to say kaddish over Myron's grave and is sharing Passover seder with her. When Tush has kittens, Mrs. Katz is thrilled to become a bubee for the first time, but not the last because by the time Larnel has grown and married, Mrs. Katz has become a member of his family and shares in the joyful birth of his children. This heart-warming story certainly proves that race, religion, and age differences need not be barriers to friendship. Polacco's dialogue-spiced text and cute drawings will make this point clear to students.

Mufaro's Beautiful Daughters: An African Tale. John Steptoe.

See page 77 for entry.

Musical Games for Children of All Ages.
Esther L. Nelson.
Illustrated by Shizu
Matsuda. Sterling
Publishing, 1976. 72
pages. (0-8069-7520-2)

Music and physical education activities can be transformed into multicultural merrymaking with the aid of this collection of songs, dances, and games. Numbering well over fifty, many of these activities require little musical ability on the teacher's part, and some of them, such as jump rope, pat-a-cake, and ball-bouncing games require none. As the Nelson reassuringly explains, "the piano arrangements in this book are as simple as possible. For many of the games you need them just to give you an idea of the tune or rhythm. . . . If you play the autoharp, the zither, the guitar or banjo, instead of (or in addition to) the piano, use them whenever you can." Some of the activities can be enjoyed by one or a small group of children while most are appropriate for whole-class participation, and there is certainly something here that will appeal to students of any age, though Nelson feels her offerings are especially appealing to 5 to 12-year-olds. The ethnic origin of every activity is not indicated; however, in many cases, the directions supply this information. To name but a few examples, there are dances such as the Russian troika, the Italian tarantella, the Swedish carousel, and the Peruvian Echunga Para La Yunga; songs such as the Ethiopian "Hoya-Hoye," the Maori "Hokoparepare," and the French "Vent Frais"; and games such as the Puerto Rican rumble to the bottom, the Chinese dragon, and the Spanish matatiru-tiru-lá.

Nessa's Fish. Nancy Luenn. Illustrated by Neil Waldman. Atheneum, 1990. 27 pages. (0-689-31477-9)

One autumn day young Nessa and her grandmother go ice fishing and catch enough to feed everyone back at camp. Tired out from their labors, they both fall asleep on the snow. When the grandmother becomes ill, Nessa protects both the fish and the old woman from the wild animals that approach in search of food. Eventually, Nessa is relieved of her guard duties when her grandfather and parents come to the rescue but nevertheless feels proud that she has successfully fulfilled her responsibilities. Waldman's soft-hued paintings of Arctic snow fields bordered by dense, ground-hugging tundra vegetation and traversed by fur-clad Native American humans, wolves, fox, and bear furnish a rather blandly told story with some culture-specific charm. Though young students may feel a bit of suspense as Nessa confronts each species of animal intruder, because she so easily dispenses with each, the excitement level is relatively low. The primary value in this book lies in the fact that it provides students with the information that even today, there are Native Americans who live in surroundings so very different from those found in the lower forty-eight states but who are, in their essential humanity, so very much like the students themselves.

Night on Neighborhood Street. Eloise Greenfield. Illustrated by Jan Spivey Gilchrist. Dial Books, 1991. 27 pages. (0-8037-0777-0)

In eighteen image-filled poems Greenfield reveals the rich texture of life in an African American neighborhood. Poems range from lullabies to honest portrayals of conflict on the street. Readers are taken inside a church and into lots of kid-populated bedrooms and living rooms. Gilchrist's luminous full-page illustrations harmonize with poems whose thematic variety is apparent from these representative samples:

Karen

Karen lets her
sister be the mama
evenings
when Mama's at work
mostly minds and
bedtimes doesn't fuss
much
just yawns wide, then waits
for her sister to tender
a mama's kiss

The Seller

when the seller comes around
carrying in his many pockets
packages of death
all the children go inside
they see behind his easy smile
they know his breath is cold
they turn their backs and
reach for warmth
and life

On the Pampas. María Cristina Brusca.

See page 78 for entry.

Panther Dream: A Story of the African Rainforest. Bob and Wendy Weir.

See page 79 for entry.

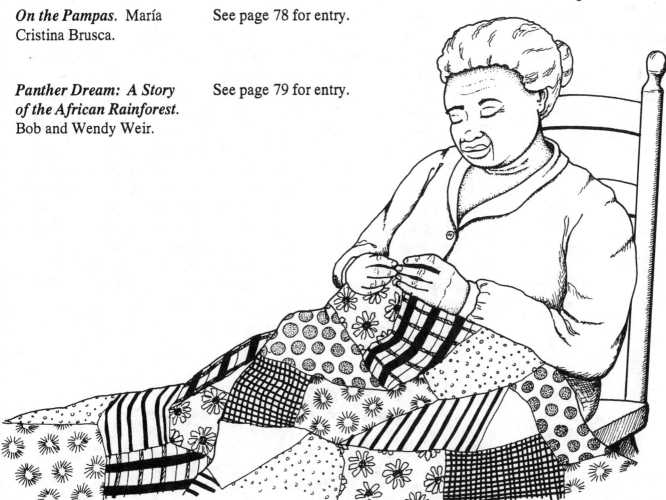

The Patchwork Quilt. Valerie Flournoy. Illustrated by Jerry Pinkney. Dial Books for Children, 1985. 29 pages. (0-8037-0097-0)

During the year it takes to complete a hand-stitched patchwork quilt, Tanya's entire family eventually gets involved, either as active participants or admiring spectators. However when Grandma had first announced her plans to assemble a masterpiece from the scrapes of the family's old clothes, no one but Tanya took much interest. But as the quilt grows, Tanya teases her mother into asking Grandma about the project, and soon the two women are spending every winter evening together cutting and stitching. Then at Christmas when Grandma becomes ill and must recover in bed for several months, Tanya takes over for her. Seeing their sister working diligently, even Ted and Jim help awhile. By late spring Grandma is well enough that Papa carries her to her chair by the window where she can enjoy some of "the Lord's light" and watch Tanya sew. One day she proclaims, "Yes, honey, this quilt is nothin' but a joy," and soon she is strong enough to put on the finishing touches herself. Pinkney's delightful paintings contribute much to a reader's understanding of the relationships between the members of Tanya's close-knit African American family. This Reading Rainbow Book and winner of the Coretta Scott King Award will encourage students to collect their own family memories in the form of scraps from favorite old clothes, blankets, or curtains and use them to construct simple but meaningful cut and glue art projects.

The People Could Fly:
American Black Folktales.
Retold by Virginia
Hamilton. Illustrated by
Leo and Diane Dillon.
Knopf, 1985. 178 pages.
(0-679-84336-1)

Says author Virginia Hamilton, "These tales were created out of sorrow. But the hearts and minds of the black people who formed them, expanded them, and passed them on to us were full of love and hope. We must look on the tales as a celebration of the human spirit." Hamilton's artistic retelling of the tales and the stunning illustrations accompanying them certainly will help readers to see this anthology as a celebration. Divided into five sections, it contains eight "Animal Tales," seven "Tales of the Real, Extravagant, and Fanciful," six "Tales of the Supernatural," and seven "Slave Tales of Freedom." The stories have been tastefully retold in moderately colloquial English that invites oral reading. Following each are some historical facts and commentary that teachers can share with their class and older students will enjoy reading themselves. Indicative of its artistry is the long list of distinguished awards this book has received: Coretta Scott King Award, An ALA *Booklist* Editors' Choice, An *SLJ* Best Book of the Year, A *Horn Book* Fanfare Honor Book, A *New York Times* Best Illustrated Book, An ALA Notable Children's Book, A Notable Children's Trade Book in the Field of Social Studies, and An NCTE Teachers' Choice.

Pettranella. Betty
Waterton. Illustrated by
Ann Blades. Douglas &
McIntyre, 1990. 26 pages.
(0-88899-108-8)

A letter from Uncle Gus, who is homesteading in Canada, convinces Pettranella's parents to leave an unnamed, smoke-filled (probably) eastern European city. Little Pettranella is thrilled at the prospect of a new land where she can have chickens and a swing and her grandmother can have "a real flower garden, not just a window box." But when the grandmother says she is too old to make the journey, Pettranella is heart-broken, so the grandmother tries to comfort her with a small muslin bag of wild flower seeds to plant in Canada. Pettranella promises to take good care of the seeds and sow them to create a garden in the grandmother's honor. Through a long sea voyage, days of waiting for homesteading papers once having arrived in Canada, and weeks of travelling by ox-cart to reach the homestead, Pettranella keeps her promise to protect the seeds. Then just a few miles from the homestead, she accidentally leaves them behind at a spot where her father stopped to fix their cart. Even after the family is settled into a newly built cabin and is enjoying the arrival of spring, Pettranella cannot help but yearn for the flower garden she had intended to plant. But joy of joys, one day when she and her parents go visiting, they happen to pass the spot where her father fixed the cart; there beside the trail are growing beautiful flowers that sprouted from the grandmother's seeds — "and to this very day, Pettranella's flowers bloom each year beside a country road in Manitoba." This sweet story adorned with equally sweet paintings presents a touching example of the strong emotional ties that exist between immigrants and the loved ones they leave behind in their native lands.

A Picture Book of Martin Luther King, Jr. David A. Adler. Illustrated by Robert Casilla. Holiday House, 1989. 28 pages. (0-8234-0770-5)

A highly informative but limited text harmonizes with evocative illustrations to produce an ideal medium for acquainting very young students with the life of Martin Luther King, Jr. A careful selection of biographical material has enabled the author to present a surprisingly well-rounded view of Dr. King without overwhelming a young audience. For instance, Adler effectively recreates the evolution of King's early passion for civil rights by describing two childhood events: King's tearful realization that two white playmates have rejected him because of his color and his experience with "White Only" signs at Atlanta parks and other public facilities. Mention of the influence on King of historical African American leaders such as Frederick Douglass, George Washington Carver, and Harriet Tubman is neatly handled by means of Casilla's captioned portraits of these three and the accompanying: "Martin learned to read at home before he was old enough to start school. All through his childhood, he read books about black leaders." Several well-chosen quotations convey in King's own words his belief in peaceful protest and his dream of racial equality. Teachers will find this book deserves multiple oral readings with plenty of time allotted for students to discuss Dr. King's accomplishments as well as to ask questions that will help them develop a rudimentary understanding of racism and the civil rights movement in America.

Rechenka's Eggs. Patricia Polacco.

See page 80 for entry.

Roberto Clemente: Baseball Superstar. Carol Greene.

See page 81 for entry.

Sachiko Means Happiness. Kimiko Sakai.

See page 82 for entry.

Sami and the Time of Troubles. Florence Parry Heide and Judith Heide Gilliland.

See page 83 for entry.

Secret Valentine. Catherine Stock. Bradbury Press, 1991. 24 pages. (0-02-788372-8)

Sweet as a candy heart, Stock's simple narrative is perfect for instilling in early primary students the true spirit of Valentine's Day. They will see that this holiday is not only a time for telling our loved ones how we care but also an occasion to reach out to those in need of friendship. Told in the first-person by a cute little African American girl, the story opens on February 8, just in time for cutting and pasting some Valentines: "Valentine's Day is coming soon. Mommy says it's a day to tell people that you love them. 'I love lots of people,' I say. 'I love you and Daddy and Grandma and Muffety.' Muffety is my cat." On the way home from purchasing doilies and colored paper, mother and daughter see an elderly neighbor who looks lonely. The little narrator decides the neighbor needs a Valentine — "I draw a rainbow on a card for the old lady next door." She mails the card off to the neighbor, and then on February 14, though the child receives many pretty cards, her favorite one smells of lavender and mysteriously reads, "From your Secret Valentine." We can assume a new intergenerational friendship has been born. Bright watercolors of the African American characters turn this into just the kind of book that should be found in all American classrooms, that is, books containing "generic American" subject matter featuring non-Anglo protagonists.

Shake It to the One That You Love the Best: Play Songs and Lullabies from Black Musical Traditions. Collected and adapted by Cheryl Warren Mattox. Illustrated by Varnette P. Honeywood and Brenda Joysmith. Warren-Mattox Productions, 1989. 56 pages. (0-9623381-0-9)

According to the preface, "this book is designed to help advance children's awareness in two aspects of Black culture — music and art," and it surely has the potential to do so. Its pages are filled with vibrant acrylics, pastels, and collages drawn from the work of two accomplished African American artists. These art works complement the musical scores of traditional favorites that have been passed down from generation to generation. These songs range from soothing lullabies to tunes that are companions to ring games (played in a circle formation), line games (children form two lines), and clapping games. Identification of origin (West Indian, African-American, Creole, etc.) and an interesting bit of history and commentary accompany each song. With a total of twenty-six songs and eleven art works, this attractive book can enrich the fine arts curriculum at any grade level, especially if used in conjunction with the tape cassette that is sold along with it.

The Snow Queen. Hans Christian Andersen. Retold by Amy Ehrlich. Illustrated by Susan Jeffers. Dial Books, 1982. 40 pages. (0-8037-0692-8)

This elegant version of Andersen's fairy tale is a feast for the eyes. Measuring 9 ½" by 12", the over-sized pages are dominated by Jeffer's gorgeous depictions of northern European forests, snow scenes, and flower-bedecked cottages as well as her fantastic representations of the trolls, talking animals, and Snow Queen who populate this story of human love and its power to overcome elemental evil. Ehrlich's graceful retelling of this Danish classic leads the reader through the adventures young Gerda experiences on her journey to find and rescue her beloved playmate Kai. Even after Kai's eye and heart have been penetrated by shards of the devil's mirror so that the world appears hideous to him and he begins to mistreat Gerda, she remains loyal. So when Kai permits himself to be lured away by the Snow Queen and everyone else has given him up for dead, Gerda sets out to find him. Surviving encounters with a witch and robbers and accepting the aid of a prince and a talking reindeer, Gerda finally locates Kai in farthest reaches of Lapland imprisoned in the Snow Queen's ice palace. A kiss from Gerda melts Kai's heart, clears his eye, and frees him from the Snow Queen's hold. The two eventually return to their village, no longer children but loving adults able to enjoy the beauty of a summer's day. An American Bookseller Pick of the Lists and a Booklist Reviewer's Choice, this work will entertain and edify readers of all ages while acquainting them with one of Denmark's best known authors.

St. Patrick's Day in the Morning. Eve Bunting. Illustrations by Jan Brett. Clarion Books, 1980. 28 pages. (0-89919-162-2)

Jamie Donovan awakes before sun up on St. Patrick's Day feeling rather dejected. Unlike the other members of his Irish family, he will not be marching in the parade to the top of Acorn Hill. Everyone says he is too small to make the long trek. But Jamie proves them wrong. Before any of his family is aware of it, he has donned his mother's raincoat, his dad's black hat, and brother Sean's green and gold sash. He then grabs brother Kevin's flute and sets out with his dog Nell to march in his very own St. Patrick's Day parade. Jamie and Nell make their way through the village where Jamie tips his hat to Kit Kelley's donkey, receives an egg from Hubble the Hen Man, irritates mad old Mrs. Mulligan with his attempts to play the flute, and is presented with a ginger ale and a miniature Irish flag by Mrs. Simms at the Half-Way-Up Sweetshop. Once out of the village, Jamie and Nell trudge up a road that winds through beautiful green meadows, and just as the sun is about to rise, they succeed in reaching the summit of Acorn Hill. Filled with subtle humor and a bit of Irish brogue, this cute story is illustrated by black, white, gold, and green drawings that will help students visualize the picturesque Irish village and countryside through which Jamie and Nell make their triumphant march.

A Story-A Story. Gale E. Haley.

See page 86 for entry.

The Talking Eggs: A Folktale from the American South. Retold by Robert D. San Souci.

See page 88 for entry.

Tar Beach. Faith Ringgold. Crown, 1991. 27 pages. (0-517-58030-6)

Derived from Ringgold's story quilt "Tar Beach," which resides in the collection of New York City's Guggenheim Museum, this autobiographically-based fantasy is a metaphor for the power the human imagination possesses to inspire. Eight-year-old Cassie Louise Lightfoot loves to spend hot summer nights on the asphalt rooftop of her Harlem apartment building, gazing up at the sky while her parents and their friends play cards. Before long, Cassie's imagination takes over and she is soaring above her new domain: "Sleeping on Tar Beach was magical. . . . I will always remember when the stars fell down around me and lifted me above the George Washington Bridge. . . . I wanted that bridge to be mine. Now I have claimed it. All I had to do was fly over it for it to be mine forever." As Cassie muses on, we learn that her dreams include freeing her dad from the discrimination that forces him to hold dangerous non-union jobs, providing her mother with a carefree life, and supplying the family with ice cream for dessert each night — all of these dreams are available to a young African American girl like Cassie, even during the 1930s, because she permits her imagination to fly among the stars. Primary students will find themselves enchanted by the luminous paintings that fill each page of this 1991 winner of the Parent's Choice Award. They surely will be encouraged to let their imaginations provide them with the kind of lofty dreams that can come true if adults help them decide what practical steps they can take to reach their goals.

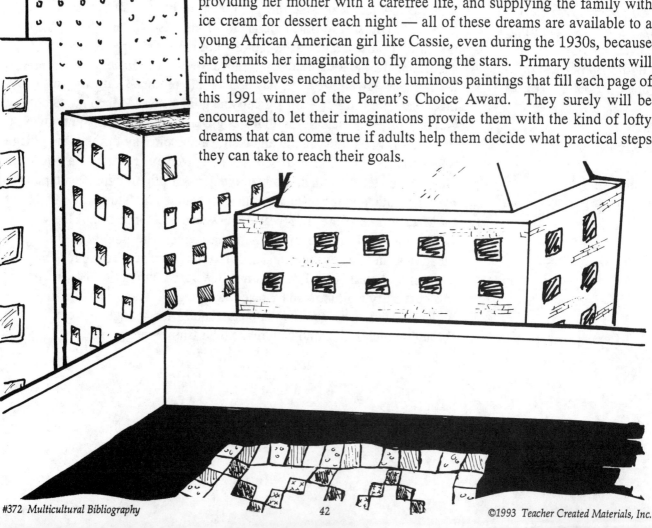

Thirteen Moons on Turtle's Back: A Native American Year of Moons. Joseph Bruchac and Jonathan London. Illustrated by Thomas Locker. Philomel Books, 1992. 32 pages. (0-399-22141-7)

"In many parts of North America, the native people relate the cycles of the moon (called Grandmother Moon by many Native Americans) to [the] seasons. In every year, there are thirteen of those moon cycles," which explains why this collection consists of thirteen free verse poems, whose substance was derived from the lore of thirteen different tribal nations — Northern Cheyenne, Potawatomi, Anishinabe, Cree, Huron, Seneca, Pomo, Menominee, Micmac, Cherokee, Winnebago, Lakota Sioux, and Abenaki. Students will find these nature poems highly accessible and full of lovely imagery. Locker's large, richly colored oil paintings will help them envision images such as those found in the first stanza of the Mimac's "Moose-Calling Moon":

> *In this season when leaves*
> *begin to turn color,*
> *we go down to the lakes*
> *and with birch-bark horns*
> *make the sound which echoes*
> *through the spruce trees,*
> *the call of a moose*
> *looking for a mate:*
> *Mooo-ahhh-ahhh*
> *Mooo-ahhh-ahhh.*

This Is the Way We Go to School: A Book About Children Around the World. Edith Baer. Illustrated by Steve Bjorkman. Scholastic, 1990. 35 pages. (0-590-43161-7)

Here is cultural diversity presented in a manner that the youngest of readers can understand and enjoy. Baer's rhyming couplets and Bjorkman's colorful cartoonish illustrations join forces to demonstrate how students living on each of the seven continents make their way to school:

> *And In Philly, Mitch and Molly*
> *go to school by trackless trolley!*
> *Bianca, Beppo, Benedetto*
> *ride aboard the vaporetto.*
> *Bundled up against the breeze,*
> *Niels and Solveig go on skis.*
> *Palm trees help keep Ahmed cool*
> *on his sunny walk to school.*

Following the main text are a listing of the homeland for each of the children mentioned in the rhymes — "Niels and Solveig live in Norway; Ahmed lives in Egypt," etc. — and a two-page world map on which the homelands have been pinpointed.

Tortillitas Para Mama and Other Nursery Rhymes/Spanish and English. Selected and translated by Margot C. Griego, et al. Illustrated by Barbara Cooney. Henry Holt, 1981. 27 pages. (0-8050-0317-7)

"These nursery rhymes and lullabies were collected from the Spanish community in the Americas. They have been passed on from generation to generation by mothers, fathers, and other family members who heard them as children and later sang them to their own children as they held them in their laps or rocked them to sleep." Besides preserving and disseminating traditional Hispanic verse, this attractive little book will help promote bilingualism among both native English and native Spanish-speaking students. Teachers will not have to work very hard to generate interest in this study tool because pre-school and early primary students will be just as enchanted by Cooney's glowing paintings as they are by the accompanying words, words such as the following, which overflow with warmth and love:

EL BESO DE MAMA
Todas las mañanas, sueño al despertar
Que un ángel del cielo me viene a besar.
Al abrir los ojos, busco adonde estoy
Y en el mismo sitio, veo a mi Mamá.

MAMA'S KISS
Every morning, I dream at dawn
That an angel from heaven will come to kiss me.
When I open my eyes, I look around
And in the same spot, I see my Mama.

The Turtle and the Island: A Folktale from Papua New Guinea. Retold by Barbara Ker Wilson. Illustrated by Frané Lessac. J. B. Lippincott, 1990. 23 pages. (0-397-32438-3)

The tropical colors of Lessac's paintings help lure the imagination back in time to the primeval waters of the South Pacific where "turtles had teeth, [and] there lived a great sea-turtle, the mother of all sea-turtles, who spent her time swimming about the wide sea." She had no choice; these were the days before the Pacific islands had been created, so the turtle could only dream of resting on a warm beach. One day, however, she came upon a large hill of sand rising from the ocean floor. When she determined that the crest of the hill nearly reached the water's surface, the turtle, bent on realizing her dream, successfully excavated rock and sand and laboriously added it to the hill until an island was born. With the help of birds who dropped seeds, the island became a lush paradise, which the turtle decided to share with the lonely man who lived deep under the ocean in a cave. To satisfy his desire for a mate, she agreed to swim to the mainland and bring him back the beautiful wife he desired. The man and woman soon produced a multitude of children and grandchildren, "and in this way the island became filled with people, who grew crops and built houses and fished along the seashore. And in time the island that the great sea-turtle had made became known as New Guinea." Older students will be able to compare this tale to creation stories from other cultures while students of all ages will be motivated to get out some maps and do some more reading to learn about present-day Papua New Guinea.

Under the Sunday Tree. Eloise Greenfield. Illustrated by Amos Ferguson. Harper Collins, 1988. 39 pages. (0-06-443257-2)

Ferguson's paintings, alive with torrid color, and Greenfield's vigorous verse together will sweep students into the tropical clime of the Bahamas. Here is but a tiny taste of this luscious collection of twenty poems:

Tradition

Pineapples! pumpkins! chickens! we

carry them on our heads you see

we can glide along forever

and not drop a thing, no never

never even use our hands

never put a finger to it

you know how we learned to do it?

knowledge came from other lands

Africans of long ago

passed it down to us and so

now we pass it on to you

for what is old is also new

pineapples, pumpkins, chickens, we

carry more than the things you see

we also carry history

Wagon Wheels. Barbara Brenner. Illustrated by Don Bolognese. Harper Trophy, 1978. 64 pages. (0-06-444052-4)

Based on information recorded in the memoirs of Lula Sadler Craig, a settler in the Kansas Territory's Nicodemus colony, *Wagon Wheels* treats a subject long ignored by TV Westerns and mainstream literature, namely the contribution newly freed African Americans made to the 19th century settlement of the West. The short sentences and elementary vocabulary of this Harper Trophy "An I Can Read Book" effectively convey the drama of the Muldie family's pioneer adventures. After a hard trek from Kentucky during which Mrs. Muldie dies, the father and three young sons survive a winter of near starvation in a Nicodemus prairie dugout (only the beneficence of the Osage Indians saves the day), a life-threatening prairie conflagration, and most amazing of all, a 150-mile journey the boys make alone on foot to meet their dad, who months before went ahead to look for a more hospitable homestead. Bolognese's sketches help to emphasize the fact that African Americans have played a variety of roles in American history. This book would make an excellent source for young students attempting some independent historical investigation.

When I Was Young in the Mountains. Cynthia Rylant. Illustrated by Diane Goode. E. P. Dutton, 1982. 27 pages. (0-525-44198-0)

Retrieved from an Appalachian childhood, the golden memories that grace the pages of this irresistible book include dinners of hot corn bread, pinto beans, and fried okra; kisses from a coal-dust laden grandfather (only his lips were clean); trips to the swimming hole for both summertime refreshment and baptisms; mornings ringing with the sound of cowbells and dusks filled with frog songs. Never mind that midnight bouts of indigestion meant trips outside to the johnny-house or that baths were taken in tubs filled with well water, which first had to be pumped and heated on the stove. The once-young girl who narrates this story of life in a vanishing American subculture has no doubt that the good outweighed the inconvenience: "When I was young in the mountains, I never wanted to go to the ocean, and I never wanted to go to the desert. I never wanted to go anywhere else in the world, for I was in the mountains. And that was always enough." Goode's sweet drawings are a wonderful addition to this glimpse at a way of life unknown to many students of today. Appropriately, this work has been designated as both a Reading Rainbow Book and a Caldecott Honor Book.

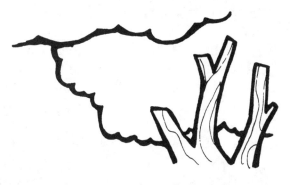

Where the Forest Meets the Sea. Jeannie Baker. Greenwillow Books, 1987. 28 pages. (0-688-06363-2)

A young boy and his father spend a sunny day together in a special part of North Queensland, Australia. "My father knows a place we can only reach by boat. Not many people go there, and you have to know the way through the reef. When we arrive, cockatoos rise from the forest in a squawking cloud. My father says there has been a forest here for over a hundred million years." (A map at the end of the book indicates the exact location of this rainforest.) Unfortunately, as the young narrator mentions later, development threatens to destroy the untouched beauty of this area. But before this gloomy thought intrudes upon the boy's excitement, he has time to wander into the rainforest where he imagines how the scene must have appeared long ago. "I find an ancient tree. It is hollow. Perhaps aboriginal forest children played here, too." Though Baker's text does a praiseworthy job of conveying the splendor of the rainforest and the pleasure the boy takes in it, her illustrations are what make this book something out of the ordinary. As she explains in the afterword, her unique "relief collages are constructed from a multitude of materials, including modeling clay, papers, textural materials, preserved natural materials, and paints." With their three-dimensional quality, these collages will give students the impression that they can step right into the forest and join the boy on his adventures. After admiring the book, students may want to gather materials and make their own collages in imitation of Baker's style.

Whistle for Willie. Ezra Jack Keats. Puffin Books, 1977. 28 pages. (0-14-050202-5)

Peter spends the day trying to accomplish one mighty task — learning how to whistle! If only he could whistle, he could call his dachshund Willie. But no mater how much he tries, poor Peter just can't get a sound to come, so he tries to forget his failures by spinning around until he' s dizzy; by hiding in an empty box; by drawing a long, long chalk line. Then, he gets the great idea of putting on his father's hat — maybe if he feels more grown up, he'll finally be able to whistle, but no such luck. Again he tries to drown his misery by walking on a crack, by running away from his shadow, even by jumping off of his shadow. When Peter spies Willie coming down the street, he decides he'll crawl under a box and try one more time: "He blew and blew and blew. Suddenly — out came a real whistle! Willie stopped and looked around to see who it was." Boy and dog run home as fast as they can to tell Peter's parents of the great occurrence. Of course, Mom and Dad simply love Peter's whistling. This is one cute book with absolutely adorable pictures of a little African American boy doing just the kind of things all children do at one time or another.

Why the Sun and the Moon Live in the Sky. Elphinstone Dayrell. Illustrated by Blair Lent. Houghton Mifflin, 1968. 27 pages. (0-395-53963-3)

Passed on by the Efik-Ibibio peoples of Southeastern Nigeria, this simple folktale portrays the sun and his wife the moon as overly generous hosts who allow themselves to be pushed right out of their earthly home by the water and all his people. The homeless couple flee to the sky where they take up permanent residence. Lent's imaginative drawings of yellow, brown, blue, and green, while not representative of the art belonging to any particular tribe, certainly help identify the story as African in origin. Teachers will find this short Caldecott Honor Book appropriate for introducing young children to the basic characteristics of the folktale genre. It could then serve as a standard against which students would compare and contrast the world view expressed in folktales from other cultures.

The Wooden Doll. Susan Bonners. Lothrop, Lee & Shepard, 1991. 29 pages. (0-688-08280-7)

A Polish nesting doll brought to America long ago by her grandfather tantalizes little Stephanie. Though her grandmother encourages her to ask for permission to play with it, she is hesitant to bother her grandfather, a man of few words who sometimes seems a little gruff. Eventually she musters the courage to speak to him but is disappointed when he tells her she is too young to handle the fragile old thing. One afternoon Stephanie's curiosity gets the better of her so that while her grandparents are napping, she retrieves the doll from a high shelf. Later she confesses her misdeed, and her grandfather, rather than showing anger, takes the opportunity to tell Stephanie about his past. He describes his life as a boy in Poland and explains that his mother received the doll as a gift from her husband on the day of his birth. When at seventeen he decided to immigrate to America, she gave it to him to take along. Stephanie drinks in the information her grandfather shares with her and feels much closer to him. He responds by deciding she is old enough to have the doll, after all. The subtle nuances Bonners develops in the relationship between grandfather and granddaughter give this story a notable charm and authenticity, which her beautiful paintings heighten.

Yagua Days. Cruz Martel. Illustrated by Jerry Pinkney. Dial Books, 1976. 35 pages. (0-8037-0457-7)

Only two days into summer vacation and time is already hanging heavy for Adan Riera. Wet weather has prevented him from playing in East Side Park, so he laments to mailman Jorge that rainy days are terrible. Trying to cheer Adan up, Jorge exclaims, "No — they're wonderful days. They're yagua days! . . . Muchacho, *this* day is a yagua day." Soon Jorge and Adan's parents are reminiscing about the fun they all had as children growing up in Puerto Rico. But Adan, a New Yorker unfamiliar with his parents' homeland, has no idea what a yagua day is and cannot share in their enthusiasm. The arrival of a letter from tío Ulise inviting Adan and his family to visit Corral Viejo lifts Adan's spirits and soon puts an end to his ignorance. The majority of this pleasant story describes the fun Adan has on his first visit to Puerto Rico where he meets his extended family, harvests fruit on his uncle's plantation, and experiences for himself the exhilaration of yagua days during which both children and adults slide down grassy, rain-slickened slopes on the coverings of palm fronds, splash-landing in the river below. Pinkey's large black and white drawings play an important role in depicting Puerto Rico's natural landscape and in conveying the warm family interactions Adan enjoys. The three dozen or so Spanish words incorporated into the dialogue add interest and appeal to the text, which with the aid of the glossary, can be enjoyed by Spanish- and non-Spanish-speaking students alike. This Reading Rainbow Book has also been designated a Notable Trade Book in the Field of Social Sciences and a Council on Interracial Books for Children Award Runner-up.

Third Through Fifth Grade

Aekyung's Dream. Min Paek. Children's Book Press, 1988. 24 pages. (0-89239-042-5)

Aekyung, having left Korea only six months earlier, is facing the problems many young immigrants encounter when beginning new lives in America: difficulty learning English, rude comments regarding appearance, multicultural ignorance among peers, and homesickness for a country where it is possible to wake up in the morning sure of what language the birds will be singing. For a time, Aekyung struggles to keep from burdening her hard-working parents with her miseries. But one morning when she awakens to the memory of a classmate's remark about her "Chinese eyes," Aekyung cannot help but tearfully exclaim to her mother, "I'm Korean, not Chinese!" Her mother tries to soothe her and does convince her she must continue going to school, but it is not until a visit from an aunt prompts Aekyung to dream of the 15th century King Sejong that she is truly comforted. Sejong tells her to be "strong like a tree" so that her "life will blossom like the mukung flower." These words and the passage of time bring about an end to Aekyung's frequent tears so that she is able to concentrate on learning English and demonstrating to her classmates that she is a proud Korean-American, not Chinese. Written in both English and Korean with vibrantly colored drawings, this book would give solace to immigrants from all cultures, as well as stimulate empathy in their otherwise potentially abusive peers.

All the Colors of the Race. Arnold Adoff.

See page 7 for entry.

An Ancient Heritage: The Arab-American Minority. Brent Ashabranner.

See page 94 for entry.

Angel Child, Dragon Child. Maria Michele Surat. Illustrated by Vo-Dinh Mai. Scholastic, 1983. 35 pages. (0-590-42271-5)

Nguyen Hoa tells of the difficulties she faces during her first year in America when she must cope not only with the absence of her mother who, for lack of money, was unable to leave Vietnam with the rest of her family, but also with the teasing of classmates. Hoa's initial stoicism gives way when the most bumptious of the teasers Raymond, "a boy with fire-colored hair," hurls a hard-packed snowball into the face of Hoa's sister. Hoa can no longer hold back her anger, retaliates with a "snowrock" of her own, and soon finds herself in a tussle with Raymond. A wise principal separates the two and confines them to a room where Hoa must use English to tell Raymond about Vietnam while Raymond must write down Hoa's life story. After a bitter silence, some tears, and a great show of magnanimity on Hoa's part, the story is written and read before the whole school at which time Raymond suggests they organize a Vietnamese fair to earn enough money to bring Hoa's mother to America. The fair is a success and eventually the Nguyen family is reunited. Pronunciation keys for the Vietnamese terms used, an afterword providing basic geographic and cultural information, and Vo-Dinh Mai's evocative colored pencil drawings all help to make this Reading Rainbow Review Book a valuable asset for developing students' understanding of and compassion for newly arrived immigrants.

The Arab Americans. Alixa Naff.

See page 94 for entry.

Arctic Explorer: The Story of Matthew Henson. Jerri Ferris.

See page 95 for entry.

Argentina. Karen Jacobsen. Childrens Press, 1990. 48 pages. (0-516-41101-2)

The geography, history, and culture of Argentina are presented in a small, light-weight paperback easier for young hands to carry than an encyclopedia volume or a typical hardcover social studies text. Printed in large type on high gloss paper and full of colorful photographs, this book would make an ideal reference source for individual or group projects focused on world cultures. Illustrative of the highly readable prose found in each of its eleven very short chapters are the exuberant opening lines of chapter one, "Argentina in the World": "Look! Hundreds of whales! Thousands of seals! More than a million penguins! Every summer, all of these animals — and more — come to the Valde's Peninsula. They come to have their babies and spend the summer. The Valde's Peninsula sticks out into the Atlantic Ocean on the east coast of Argentina. Argentina is the eighth largest country in the world." Succeeding chapters provide basic facts about Argentina's four major geographic regions — the Andes, the North, the Patagonia, and the Pampa; native peoples, European settlement, and the fight for independence; and life in Argentina today — education, popular foods and sports, and holidays. A list of "Words You Should Know" and a short index conclude this handsome little book.

Bernardo de Gálvez.
Frank de Varona.
Illustrated by Tom
Redman. Steck-Vaughn,
1991. 32 pages.
(0-8114-6756-2)

De Varona, as author of this particular volume and general consulting editor for the series, addresses his readers in an opening message: "The books in this series include Hispanics from the United States, Spain, and Latin America, as well as from other countries. . . . [Their] contributions were a part of the development of the United States and its rich and varied cultural heritage. These Hispanics had one thing in common. They had goals, and they did whatever was necessary to achieve those goals, often against great odds. What we see in these people are dedicated, energetic men and women who had the ability to change the world to make it a better place. They can be your role models." In the case of this individual book, the role model comes in the form a man born during the mid-eighteenth century in a village near Málaga, Spain, who was to accomplish much in his forty years. A popular leader known for his compassion, Bernardo de Gálvez fought bravely for his country in the New World, in the process contributing to the American victory in the Revolution, and governed a variety of territories that encompassed parts of present-day Mexico, Cuba, Louisiana, and Florida. Bold, colorful illustrations and a text written in both Spanish and English make this book an attractive aid to developing cultural pride in Hispanic students.

Best-Loved Folktales of the World. Selected and with an introduction by Joanna Cole.

See page 11 for entry.

The Biographical Dictionary of Black Americans. Rachel Kranz.

See page 97 for entry.

Birthday. John Steptoe.
Henry Holt, 1972. 29
pages. (0-8050-1849-2)

Written in Black English Vernacular and set in the imaginary separatist community of Yoruba, this is a birthday story meant to instill cultural pride in young African American readers. The story opens on the morning of Javaka Shatu's eighth birthday. Javaka tells us that he and his birthday are very important to his community. As the firstborn of Yoruba, he is "the first child of a whole new thing," the "new thing" being an agricultural settlement begun by Javaka's dad and his friends. Named after the Yoruba people of Africa, this settlement embodies hope and pride for Javaka: "My

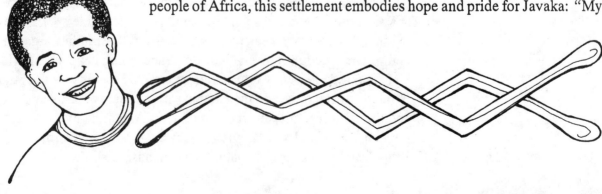

Daddy always tells me about the time before we came here to live and the old America, where him and my Mamma used to live at. He says the people there didn't treat him like a man 'cause he was Black. That seemed stupid to me 'cause my Daddy is the strongest and smartest man alive. . . . When I grow up, I'm gonna be strong like my Daddy." At Javaka's party adults and children alike enjoy a rollicking good time: "They had steel drums and bongos and horns that the men played. The music was boss, everybody was dancin' and singin' and the grown-ups was drinkin' rum and stuff." During a serious moment following a prayer, Javaka makes his birthday wish: "I said something real corny but I meant it anyway. 'I hope that we all can live together like this forever.'" John Steptoe, author/illustrator of two Caldecott Honor Books, has adorned this special book with luxuriously colorful art work.

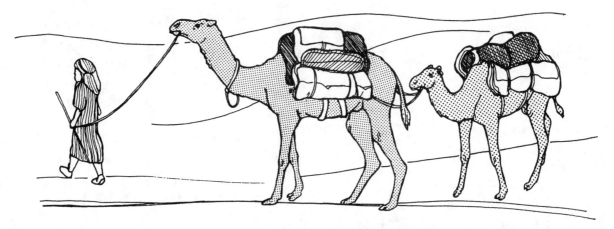

Camels Can Make You Homesick and Other Stories. Nazneen Sadiq. Illustrated by Mary Cserepy. James Lorimer & Co., 1985.
(0-88862-912-5)

The five light-hearted short stories found in this collection take a look at early adolescence from a bicultural perspective. The young protagonists wrestle with situations that arise from their special status as Canadian citizens whose parents were born and raised on the Indian subcontinent. For instance, there is Shanaz, the daughter of Pakistani parents, who suffers both pride and embarrassment after showing up at her middle school with hands dyed a bright henna orange — she let her neighbor paint beautiful designs on her hands as part of the Muslim Eid festivities, never dreaming that the dye would not wash off for a whole month! Amit has a slightly different problem; he feels quite comfortable being a Canadian kid who enjoys both hamburgers and the delicious Indian pastries called gulab jamuns. What he finds so troublesome is the arrival of Dida, the Bengali grandmother he has never met. When she comes to Canada for a visit, Amit feels a bit put off by her behavior and appearance. But then one night when his family takes Dida to McDonald's for dinner, Amit has the chance to impress her with his expertise on North American cuisine — milk shakes, Big Macs, and Chicken McNuggets. From then on, Amit and Dida get along just fine. Each of the five stories in this slim volume will amuse students as well as increase their cultural awareness, particularly regarding Indian, Pakistani, and Islamic traditions.

The Caribbean: The Land and Its People. Eintou Pearl Springer.

See page 98 for entry.

The Children of Nepal. Reijo Harkonen.

See page 13 for entry.

Children of Promise: African-American Literature and Art for Young People. Charles Sullivan.

See page 99 for entry.

Children of the Yukon. Ted Harrison.

See page 14 for entry.

The Children's Jewish Holiday Kitchen. Joan Nathan.

See page 14 for entry.

The Chinese Mirror. Mirra Ginsburg.

See page 15 for entry.

Cornrows. Camille Yarbrough. Illustrated by Carole Byard. Coward-McCann, 1979. 42 pages. (0-698-20529-4)

When caressed by the loving hands and voices of Mama and Great-Grammaw, Sister and her little brother are treated not only to elegant new hairdos but also to a lively, rhythmic lesson on the African origins of cornrow braids. Overflowing each page of this richly textured story are cultural pride and intergenerational warmth: "Child, come an sit by my knee,/an I will tell you about your family tree./An I will dress you/as a prince should be,/an the right name will come to both you an me./An I will braid your hair. . . ." Once each braid has been securely fastened into a *suku* — the Yoruba term for "basket" — the children must name their cornrows. Mama helps by chanting the possibilities, which include a veritable *Who's Who* of African American heros. Byard's black and white portraits capture the joy, the dignity, the accomplishment, and the pain which have informed the African American experience. To deepen their understanding of African American history and culture, during post-reading activities students might explore some of the many potential research topics *Cornrows* touches upon.

54

Count Your Way through the Arab World. Jim Haskins. Illustrated by Dana Gustafson. Carolrhoda Books, 1991. 22 pages. (0-87614-487-3)

Every couple of pages, one of the first ten Arabic numbers is introduced along with its pronunciation and a short article discussing some aspect of Arab culture. Though the inclusion of each number in the accompanying article has often been rather awkwardly accomplished, students will nevertheless have fun learning to count in Arabic as well as pick up some interesting facts from Haskins' clearly written prose. They will learn, for example, what significance Mecca, the Kaaba, prayer, Muhammad, and Allah have for the ninety percent of Arabs who are Muslims. They will also read about the extended families, modes of transportation, major products, and geography that are common to the countries which comprise the Arab-speaking world, which is clearly delineated in a map. This brief, colorfully illustrated work would serve as a good basic source of information for students not yet ready for tackling lengthier, more detailed discussions of Arab culture such as those found in an encyclopedia.

Count Your Way through China. Jim Haskins. Illustrated by Dennis Hockerman. Carolrhoda Books, 1987. 22 pages. (0-87614-486-5)

Every couple of pages, one of the first ten Chinese numbers is introduced along with its pronunciation and a short article discussing some aspect of Chinese culture. Though the inclusion of each number in the accompanying article has often been rather awkwardly accomplished, students will nevertheless have fun learning to count in Chinese, as well as pick up some interesting facts from Haskins' clearly written prose. They will learn, for example, a little about the ten major Chinese dynasties, the art of making porcelain, and the history of the Great Wall. They will also be introduced to China's creation myth, five-tone musical scale, and seven climatic zones. The division of China into the mainland People's Republic and Taiwan is clearly delineated in a map. This brief, colorfully illustrated book would serve as a good basic source of information for students not yet ready for tackling lengthier, more detailed discussions of Chinese culture such as those found in an encyclopedia.

Count Your Way through Japan. Jim Haskins. Illustrated by Martin Skoro. Carolrhoda Books, 1987. 22 pages. (0-87614-485-7)

Every couple of pages, one of the first ten Japanese numbers is introduced along with its pronunciation and a short article discussing some aspect of Japanese culture. Though the inclusion of each number in the accompanying article has often been rather awkwardly accomplished, students will nevertheless have fun learning to count in Japanese, as well as pick up some interesting facts from Haskins' clearly written prose. They will learn, for example, a little about Mt. Fuji's geology and history, the use of chopsticks, the design of *kimonos*, and the characteristics of *No* theater. They will also be introduced to *Sumo* wrestling, the art of calligraphy, and the political divisions of the Japanese Islands, which are clearly delineated in a map. The "Introductory Note" provides a simple but informative explanation of the Chinese origins of the Japanese writing and number systems. This brief, colorfully illustrated book would serve as a good basic source of information for students not yet ready for tackling lengthier, more detailed discussions of Japanese culture such as those found in an encyclopedia.

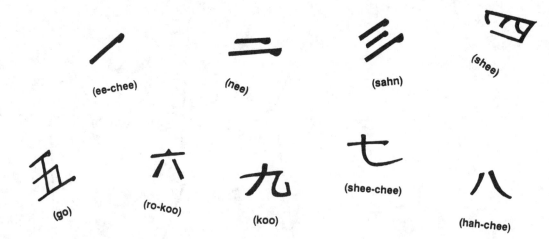

Count Your Way through Mexico. Jim Haskins. Illustrated by Helen Byers. Carolrhoda Books, 1989. 22 pages. (0-87614-349-4)

Every couple of pages, one of the first ten Spanish numbers is introduced along with its pronunciation and a short article discussing some aspect of Mexican culture. Though the inclusion of each number in the accompanying article has often been rather awkwardly accomplished, students will nevertheless have fun learning to count in Spanish as well as pick up some interesting facts from Haskins' clearly written prose. They will learn, for example, a little about indigenous edible plants, the ancient Pyramid of the Sun, and the conquest of the Aztecs by the Spanish conquistadores. They will also be introduced to the Mexican War, the volador (or flying pole dance), and Mexican arts and crafts. In addition, the "Introductory Note" provides some basic information about the languages that are spoken in Mexico today — about fifty Indian languages/dialects and a variety of Spanish called *el canto Mexicano*. This brief, colorfully illustrated book would serve as a good elementary source of information for students not yet ready for tackling lengthier, more detailed discussions of Mexican culture such as those found in an encyclopedia.

Dancing Teepees: Poems of American Indian Youth. Virginia Driving Hawk Sneve, editor and contributor. Illustrated by Stephen Gammell. Holiday House, 1989. 32 pages. (0-8234-0724-1)

A collection of poetry easily understood by primary students but appealing to all, this brightly illustrated anthology reflects both traditional and contemporary Native American concerns. So often, as in the following example, a poem of only a few lines summons up vivid images that students will want to translate into paintings and drawings of their own:

Nicely, nicely, nicely, away in the east,
the rain clouds care for the little corn plants
as a mother cares for her baby

— Zuni Corn Ceremony

In an introductory note, anthologist Virginia Driving Hawk Sneve helps the reader appreciate the artistry involved in the creation of these lovely works : "To American Indians, the spoken word was sacred. Children listened to their grandparents tell stories, recite ceremonial prayers and chants, and sing lullabies and other tribal songs. The children grew up remembering this music and knew that the act of speaking words gave life to Native American stories, songs, and prayers. Words were chosen carefully and never wasted. Many of the selections here have been passed from the old to the young. Others are from contemporary tribal poets. . ., who, as children, learned to respect the power of the spoken word." This collection will surely help instill both love and respect for language in children of all racial backgrounds as well as give them a better understanding of Native American culture.

Diego. Jonah Winter. Illustrated by Jeanette Winter. Translated from English by Amy Prince. Knopf, 1991. 32 pages. (0-679-81987-8)

This biography of acclaimed Mexican muralist Diego Rivera concentrates on his early years but follows his development into an adult artist. After the death of his twin brother, Diego was sent to live for a while with Antonia, an Indian healer. As a homecoming present, his parents gave him some colored chalk, and before long, the young child's passion for drawing was evident: "Diego drew everywhere, even on the walls. He loved to draw so much, his father made him a studio. The walls were covered with blackboards. Diego drew and drew and drew, making murals that covered the whole room." The dreamy budding artist had difficulty with his studies, so his parents sent him to art school. But even art school was not for Diego — he grew tired of drawing exercises and wanted to go out into the world to paint reality. Soon he was devoting his talents to depicting his favorite subject matter, the Mexican people. On a trip to Italy, he marvelled at the murals he saw displayed on the walls of churches and was moved to begin work on his own. "He put everything he'd ever seen into them — things from Antonia's hut, things from the Day of the Dead, the fiestas, scenes from the desert, from the jungle. . . Everything. His murals were huge. There was nothing else like them in the world." Written in both English and Spanish and bursting with color supplied by Jeanette Winter's illustrations, this winner of the 1991 Parents' Choice award will inspire art projects, foster bilingualism, and encourage students to visit the library to find books containing examples of Rivera's work.

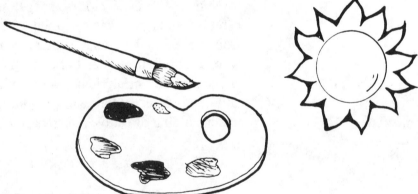

Down Under: Vanishing Cultures. Jan Reynolds. Harcourt, 1992. 32 pages. (0-15-224183-3)

On Bathhurst Island just off the north coast of Australia lives a group of aborigines called the Tiwi. Believing that "the loss of the Tiwi's traditional way of life is our loss, too," photographer Jan Reynolds spent some time with two Tiwi women and a young girl named Amprenula so as to capture something of their culture. Based on observations made as Reynolds accompanied Amprenula and the women on a "walkabout," this book presents a fascinating glimpse into a society that seems to have remained relatively unchanged by developments in the modern world. On this walkabout, a religious as well as physical journey, Amprenula takes part in the constant foraging for food such as snakes, rodents, worms, and turtle eggs. In the process, she melds spiritually with the natural world and its original creators, especially when she performs ritual movements known as "dancing her Dreaming." And like children the world round, Amprenula loves cooling off in the river and swimming at the beach, only in

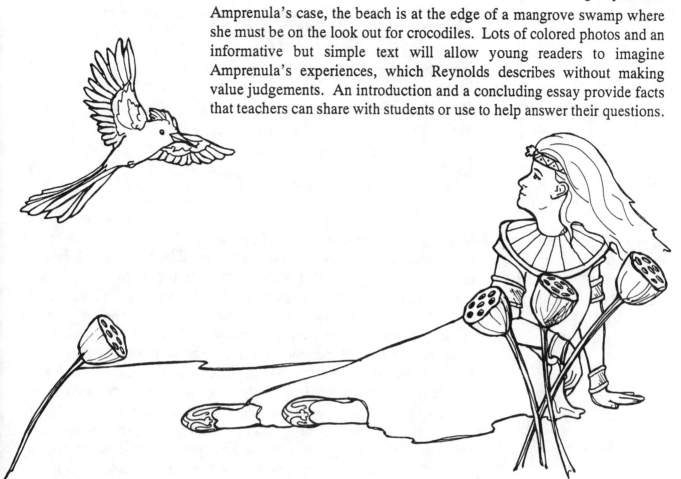

Amprenula's case, the beach is at the edge of a mangrove swamp where she must be on the look out for crocodiles. Lots of colored photos and an informative but simple text will allow young readers to imagine Amprenula's experiences, which Reynolds describes without making value judgements. An introduction and a concluding essay provide facts that teachers can share with students or use to help answer their questions.

The Egyptian Cinderella. Shirley Climo. Illustrated by Ruth Heller. Harper Trophy, 1989. 29 pages. (0-06-443279-3)

In the "Author's Note," Climo explains that "the tale of Rhodopis and the rose-red slippers is one of the world's oldest Cinderella stories. It was first recorded by the Roman historian Strabo in the first century B.C. The story is both fact and fable. . . . What *is* fact is that a Greek slave girl, Rhodopis, married the Pharaoh Amasis (Dynasty XXVI, 570-526 B.C.) and became his queen." In Climo's version of the story, Rhodopis (meaning rosy-cheeked in Greek) suffers the taunts of the household servant girls each day as she washes clothes and gathers reeds in the waters of the Nile. The lonely Rhodopis seeks companionship among the animals, and one evening when she is entertaining the birds and monkeys and hippos, her master catches sight of her dancing. Captivated by her airy grace, he decides to give her a pair of dainty slippers. The servant girls are filled with jealously and thus take special pleasure in leaving Rhodopis behind to work as they pole their raft towards Memphis to attend the Pharaoh's feast. But before the girls can even reach their destination, the feast is called to a halt when a falcon shows up carrying one of Rhodopis' slippers; the Pharaoh, who is bored by the festivities and enchanted by the tiny shoe, decides he will immediately begin a search for the owner of the slipper, hoping to make her his wife. The story ends with the Pharaoh leading Rhodopis to the royal barge. Richly hued drawings filled with papyrus and lotus blossoms emphasize the geographic setting of a tale that students will surely find familiar yet intriguingly exotic.

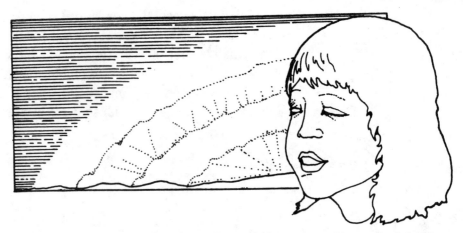

Elfwyn's Saga. David Wisniewski. Lothrop, Lee & Shepard, 1990. 29 pages. (0-688-09589-5)

Stunning cut-paper illustrations of the Far North and its early inhabitants complement an exciting original tale informed by Icelandic history and legend. The trouble begins when Gorm the Grim — the quintessential vicious Viking — carves a runic curse into a boulder overlooking a prized valley that his rival Anlaf has claimed ahead of him. The curse dooms Anlaf's soon-to-be-born child to blindness. When the baby arrives, the midwives believe that she should receive the customary treatment afforded the handicapped and mutter to Anlaf, "This is an ill omen. . . . Such a one should not be permitted to live. Better to let the snow be its blanket." But Anlaf welcomes the child, naming her Elfwyn, Celtic for "beloved of the elves." Appropriately named, Elfwyn is under the constant protection of the Hidden Folk and grows into a sprightly child seemingly immune to harm. Eventually with the elves' help, Elfwyn rids the land of Gorm and his evil magic crystal, which she shatters into fragments that fly into the heavens and produce the Northern Lights. In the process, the curse of blindness is dispelled and Elfwyn gains sight. An informative author's note offers background that both enriches the story and is likely to spur students' interest in researching Icelandic culture, but maybe most important is the potential this book has for opening up discussion of the valuable roles the physically handicapped can play in any society.

Elinda Who Danced in the Sky: An Estonian Folktale. Adapted by Lynn Moroney. Illustrated by Veg Reisberg. Children's Book Press, 1990. 32 pages. (0-89239-066-2)

A strong female character is the protagonist of this folktale whose origin is found in the epic poem of Estonia, *The Kalevipoeg*. Elinda's story begins "long ago in a land far to the north" when she hatches from a tiny egg and takes on the job of caring for the birds by guiding them to the "special sky path" along which they migrate. Elinda is adored by all, so when she reaches a marriageable age, she has no shortage of suitors. The earthly suitors, Elinda rejects out of hand. And though apparently attracted to North Star, the Moon, and the Sun, she wisely rejects each of them as well: as she reasonably concludes, "North Star would always be distant and unmoving and I would have to stay in the same place all the time"; "Moon travels, but he always takes the same narrow path"; and "Sun's light is too harsh. I would have to hide from his glare, always living in his shadow. My own light would never be seen." Finally, Elinda does find what she believes would be the perfect mate in Prince Borealis and begins weaving her wedding veil. But she weaves and she weaves until her veil reaches the end of the earth and still the prince does not return. Once she has recovered from her disappointment, her faithful feathered friends lift her into the sky, crown her with the stars, and make her queen of the sky where her veil drifts along and is called the Milky Way. The rich colors of Reisburg's illustrations add further charm to this delightful Eastern European tale.

An Ellis Island Christmas. Maxinne Rhea Leighton.

See page 20 for entry.

Ellis Island: New Hope in a New Land. William Jay Jacobs. Scribner's, 1990. 34 pages. (0-684-19171-7)

An interesting account of the role Ellis Island played in the history of American immigration, this nonfictional work contains numerous photographs of the courageous Europeans who left their homelands behind during the late nineteenth and early twentieth centuries to seek a better life in America. Divided into five short chapters, the book opens with a present-tense narrative that takes readers back to March 27, 1907, the day of arrival for 16,050 immigrants, the greatest number ever to have arrived in one day. The narrative recreates the exciting, harrowing, and sometimes heartbreaking experience of undergoing the psychological and physical examinations that determined whether a newcomer would be accepted and permitted to leave Ellis Island for the mainland or rejected and shipped back to Europe. Subsequent chapters briefly trace the history of immigration to North America and then focus on the story of Ellis Island itself. Originally called Gull Island by Native Americans, the island later became the site where the British hanged pirates, served as the location of Samuel Ellis's tavern, provided storage for weapons during the War of 1812 and the Civil War, and finally was sold to the U.S. government and opened its doors to immigrants on January 1, 1892. The author concludes with a short discussion of Ellis Island's present status an a national monument that commemorates the courage of all immigrants, European and otherwise. Highly informative and nicely written, this book will remind students that the immigrant experience is part of each of our pasts, whether quite recent or more distant.

Eyes of the Dragon.
Margaret Leaf. Illustrated
by Ed Young. Lothrop,
Lee & Shepard, 1987. 29
pages. (0-688-06155-9)

Inspired by the work of thirteenth century artist Ch'en Jung, the author has produced a fable set "long ago in faraway China" which demonstrates the dangers of excessive pride. A magistrate persuades his people to build a high wall around their village to protect them from wild beasts and evil spirits. Extremely proud of the wall, the magistrate is horrified to find his young grandson Li marking upon it. When the boy explains he is only trying to decorate the plain surface, the magistrate decides to hire the famous dragon painter Ch'en Jung to beautify the wall and thus glorify himself. Jung agrees to paint a huge dragon but only under two conditions: first, that he receive forty silver coins, which he will donate to followers of the Tao and second, that his creation be accepted without criticism. The magistrate agrees and work begins. But when he has completed his magnificent painting, Jung is dismayed to learn the magistrate will not hand over the coins until Jung adds eyes to the dragon's face. Despite Jung's warning, the magistrate insists on the eyes. Almost immediately, the dragon comes to life and with a terrible scream flees to the heavens, destroying the wall in the process. Students will be taken with Ed Young's vivid pastel illustrations and, after some research into the art of Chinese dragon painting, may want to create a dragon of their own stretching the length of a classroom wall, but will they dare give it eyes?

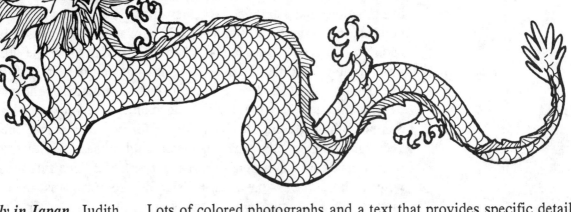

A Family in Japan. Judith
Elkin. Photography by
Stuart Atkin. Lerner
Publications, 1987. 32
pages. (0-8225-1672-1)

Lots of colored photographs and a text that provides specific detail will help acquaint students with life in Japan. They will meet Daisuke, a twelve-year-old sixth grader, and accompany him and members of his family as they go about their daily activities in Higashi Matsuyama, a suburb of Tokyo. In the process, they will learn a number of interesting facts regarding Japanese culture. For instance, in a passage describing a typical school day, young readers will discover something about the challenges involved in mastering the Japanese language: "One of the hardest things Daisuke studies is the Japanese language. To be able to read and write it properly, he has to learn two thousand characters (called *kanji*) and two forty-eight-letter alphabets called *hiragana* and *katakana*. Each kanji has to be written in a very particular way: in the right order and in the right direction using a thin brush and ink." A pronunciation guide, maps, and a table of facts about Japan are nice additions to an already fact-filled book, which is part of the series *Families the World Over*. Included in this series are more than two dozen books that explore family life in a wide variety of cultures.

Favorite Tales from Many Lands. Walter Retan.

See page 23 for entry.

Filipinos. Jodine Mayberry. Franklin Watts, 1990. 64 pages. (0-531-10978-X)

This book gives recognition to a group of Americans which has not often enjoyed the spotlight: "Filipinos have been nearly invisible to most Americans. People mistake them for Chinese, Japanese, and Mexicans. They are most often taken for Hispanics because of their Spanish surnames and because many of them speak Spanish. But Filipinos are proud of their culture and heritage. They want to be recognized as Filipinos." A careful reading of Mayberry's work, part of the series *Recent American Immigrants*, will help students appreciate the unique culture and history that distinguish Filipino Americans from other Americans. For example, they will discover that Illocano — not Tagalog-based Pilipino — is the language most often spoken by immigrants to the U.S. They will be able to understand the tragic irony behind the fact that even when the Philippines were owned by the U.S. and thus Filipinos were free to come to mainland U.S.A., they were all-to-often rejected by fellow Americans. They will learn that Filipino doctors and nurses have made significant contributions to American medicine, during the 1980s in particular. In other words, this well-researched book with its many photographs and frequent use of quotations will provide students with important facts about a population that is "expected to be the largest Asian group in the United States by the end of the century."

The Flute Player: An Apache Folktale. Michael Lacapa. Northland Publishing, 1990. 43 pages. (0-87358-500-3)

As a boy, artist Michael Lacapa listened to the White Apache storytellers from whom he learned the haunting story of a youth and maiden whose deep love still reverberates along the canyon where they courted long ago. Lacapa's richly illustrated, unadorned retelling of this tale begins at a hoop dance where the youth and maiden, as all observers can tell, fall instantly for one another. Thereafter, each day the boy plays for the girl on his flute a tune of such delicacy that the people working nearby in the canyon say, "Listen, that sounds like the wind blowing through the trees." But the girl knows that the beautiful sound is music created in her honor and signals her love and admiration by plucking a leaf from a tree and letting it float down the river where the boy receives it and accurately interprets its meaning. All is well until the boy must join his elders on a hunting expedition. In his absence, the girl, deprived of his music, succumbs to love sickness. Upon the boy's return, he learns of the girl's death and soon disappears forever, but even to this day, when the native people listen to the echoes of the canyon, they smile to themselves in the knowledge that the girl hears the exquisite melody and still loves her flute player. Pure enjoyment and an appreciation for the universality of the emotions of love and grief are sure to come to students who experience Lacapa's book.

Follow the Drinking Gourd. Jeanette Winter. Knopf, 1988. 44 pages. (0-679-81997-5)

Powerfully transmitted by Winter's paintings and text are the daring and ingenuity of both the slaves who escaped along the famous Underground Railway and the abolitionist guides, or conductors, who lead them towards freedom. As the title for her book, Winter took the name of an actual song that played a surprisingly important role in the success of the Underground Railroad. In a prefatory note this role is explained: "Among [the] conductors, there was a one-legged sailor named Peg Leg Joe. Joe hired himself out to plantation owners as a handyman. Then he made friends with the slaves and taught them what seemed a harmless folk song — "Follow the Drinking Gourd." But hidden in the lyrics of the song were directions for following the Underground Railroad. The Drinking Gourd is the Big Dipper, which points to the North Star." In Winter's fictionalized account of the escape of five slaves, the song successfully directs them to a spot on the Ohio River where Joe is waiting with a boat. "Under a starry sky Joe rowed them across the wide Ohio River. He told them of hiding places where they would be safe." With the aid of many brave white friends, the five former slaves eventually are successful in making their way into Canada. The music and lyrics to the song that inspired and guided so many are found on the last page of a book worthy of being incorporated into the social studies curriculum at all elementary schools.

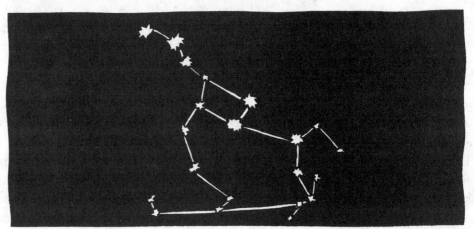

The Fool and the Fish: A Tale from Russia. Alexander Nikolayevich Afanasyev. Retold by Lenny Hort. Illustrated by Gennady Spirin. Dial Books, 1990. 22 pages. (0-8037-0861-0)

Lively humor pervades Hort's rendering of this tale by Alexander Nikolayevich Afanasyev, "a reteller of Russian folktales, [occupying] a place in the USSR comparable to the Brothers Grimm in the West." The story follows the exploits of lazy Ivan — brother to Yasha and Sasha, who are married to Masha and Dasha. Only with great urging and the lure of a pair of green boots can anybody get Ivan to help with the household chores. One day with the vision of the boots dancing in his head to motivate him, Ivan drags himself away from his bed on top of the fireplace to retrieve a couple of pails of water. When he discovers a magnificent pike in one of the pails, all he can think of is fish soup. "Don't be a fool," the pike admonishes. "Throw me back, and every wish you ever make will come true." Ivan tosses back the fish but is so foolish that he doesn't even bother to consider the value of the powers he now possesses. Instead, he makes a series of haphazard wishes solely for the purpose of saving himself a little exertion and as a result, causes others lots of trouble. Finally, however, he manages to win the Tsar's favor, marry the princess — which the whole country celebrates with vodka and fish — and live happily ever after. The stylish illustrations of celebrated Soviet artist Gennady Spirin will give students a glimpse of life in Tsarist Russia as well as add to their amusement.

Fortune. Diane Stanley.

See page 100 for entry.

The Friendship. Mildred D. Taylor.

See page 101 for entry.

Games of the World: How to Make Them, How to Play Them, How They Came to Be, Swiss Committee for UNICEF.

See page 25 for entry.

The Girl Who Changed Her Fate: A Retelling of a Greek Folktale. Laura Marshall.

See page 102 for entry.

A Greek Potter. Giovanni Caselli.

See page 104 for entry.

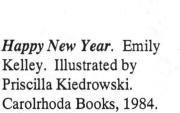

Happy New Year. Emily Kelley. Illustrated by Priscilla Kiedrowski. Carolrhoda Books, 1984. 48 pages. (0-87614-469-5)

From this book, readers of all ages could undoubtedly acquire much new information regarding the variety of customs involved in celebrating New Years the world over; however, simple sentence structure, pronunciation guides, and a glossary make this work particularly appropriate for young students embarking upon their first multicultural studies. A surprisingly large number of facts is presented in the several pages of text and pictures devoted to the customs associated with each of the seven countries featured: Ecuador, Iran, Japan, Israel, Vietnam, Sierra Leone, and China. Following the main text are a map and thumb-nail sketches highlighting interesting tidbits about New Years as celebrated in Belgium, France, Switzerland, Puerto Rico, Spain, and Greece. In addition, the book concludes with a New Years resolution game, riddles, a recipe for wassail, and a traditional English tune sung by the boys of Merry Old England who would go "wassailing the fruit trees" on New Years Day.

Hawaii Is a Rainbow.
Stephanie Feeney.

See page 26 for entry.

*Hello, My Name Is
Scrambled Eggs*. Jamie
Gilson.

See page 106 for entry.

*Hershel and the
Hanukkah Goblins*. Eric
Kimmel. Illustrated by
Trina Schart Hyman.
Holiday House, 1989. 30
pages. (0-8234-0769-1)

In this fanciful tale, Hershel of Ostropol demonstrates courage, cunning, and religious devotion when he volunteers to confront the evil goblins who have prevented the villagers from celebrating Hanukkah by snuffing candles, breaking dreidels, and hurling potato latkes to the floor. In order to dispel the goblins' power, Hershel must spend eight nights alone in the old synagogue on the hill, seeing to it that each night the menorah is lit. Most challenging of all, on the eighth night he must trick the king of the goblins himself into lighting the Hanukkah candles. Much enhanced by Hyman's imaginative drawings, each confrontation with one of the goofy but threatening-looking beasts may produce more smiles than awe in student readers. Nevertheless, Hershel's undertaking, which in the end enables the spirit of Hanukkah to triumph, carries with it an important message regarding perseverance in the fight for religious freedom. Concluding with a brief discussion of the origin and traditions of Hanukkah, this book will arouse students' interest in other Jewish traditions and stimulate their desire to study the historical and contemporary struggles against religious persecution that have been carried on by believers of many different faiths.

*Himalaya: Vanishing
Cultures*. Jan Reynolds.
Harcourt, 1991. 32 pages.
(0-15-234466-7)

Why bother learning about cultures far removed from our own? Author/photographer Jan Reynolds in the introduction to this brief examination of Himalayan society provides the answer: "Although Sherpas and the Tibetans may appear different from us, we all share the same feelings and basic needs. We really are all alike no matter where we live. We all belong to the same family, the human family, and every time a culture disappears, we lose a part of ourselves. Because of this, perhaps we should take a look at life in the Himalaya before it vanishes forever." Reynolds offers just that opportunity. Having taken her camera to the mountainous village of Namche Bazaar, Nepal, she is able to introduce us to a young Sherpa girl named Yangshi whose great grandfather came from Tibet. We learn about the activities Yangshi and her family engage in on a typical day, which begins with a cup of chia — a warm milky tea. Usually a trip is made to the village so that Yangshi's mother can sell or trade homemade goods such as rice drink. Sometimes Yangshi and her sister accompany their father to the monastery where they enjoy spinning the prayer wheels. Yangshi's chores include helping in the vegetable garden, doing laundry in a tub, and carding wool. Yangshi also helps care for her family's Yaks, a vital form of transportation as well as a food source. Students will enjoy Reynold's simple but engaging narrative, breath-taking photos of the mountains, and expressive portraits of Yangshi and her fellow Sherpas.

Hoang Anh: A Vietnamese-American Boy. Diane Hoyt-Goldsmith. Photography by Lawrence Migdale. Holiday House, 1992. 32 pages. (0-8234-0948-1)

"My name is Hoang Anh Chau. I live in the town of San Rafael, California. In our home, we speak two languages: Vietnamese and English. I came to this country with my family when I was just a baby. We are all refugees from Vietnam, here to begin a new life." With this greeting and a large photo featuring Hoang's winning smile, readers are introduced to a middle school student who not only survives but actually relishes his bi-cultural life. Hoang continues his story with a rather detailed description of his family's 1978 escape from Vietnam as "boat people." Then he explains what family life is like in America where, though Hoang also likes pizza, Vietnamese dishes are his favorites; football is his preferred pass time and a possible career goal; and English is a tongue that must be managed with some difficulty because it is "quite different" from Vietnamese, a tonal language. In his discussion of TET, the Vietnamese New Year during which he and his family enjoy celebrating their heritage, Hoang retells a legend explaining why *banh day* (rice cakes) are an important part of the festivities and reports on the TET festival held at the fairgrounds in San Jose. Though presented as a first-person narrative, Hoyt-Goldsmith's fact-filled text is obviously a condensed and polished version of what interviews with Hoang and research have provided. Lots of colorful photographs, a glossary, and a map of Southeast Asia complete this solid introduction to the Vietnamese-American experience.

Hopscotch Around the World. Mary D. Lankford. Illustrated by Karen Milone. Morrow, 1992. 48 pages. (0-688-08419-2)

Of what real importance is a book about nineteen different versions of hopscotch? Well, besides offering lots of possibilities for having some plain old fun, Lankford's carefully researched work will help students feel a kinship with children the world round who share their love of this ancient game. In existence for at least two millennia, hopscotch is thought to have been introduced to the British by Roman soldiers. This and lots of other choice tidbits that will interest hopscotch enthusiasts are to be found within the pages of this well-designed book. Accompanying the entry for each of the nineteen games is a diagram of the pattern to be traced on the ground, a detailed set of instructions, a colorful illustration featuring children from a particular country playing their variety of hopscotch, and a handful of facts relating the game to its culture of origin. For instance, in regard to *jumby*, the version of hopscotch played by the children of Trinidad, readers will learn the following: "*Jumby*, a word used by English-speaking people of the Caribbean islands, means 'spirit' or 'ghost.' Another word for *jumby* is *duppy*. On the island of Trinidad in the West Indies, over one-third of the people are of black African ancestry. Perhaps they brought the word *jumby* with them when they came from Africa to this island." Older students will have fun reading through this book themselves while teachers will appreciate it as a source of games that can be enjoyed by both primary and intermediate students.

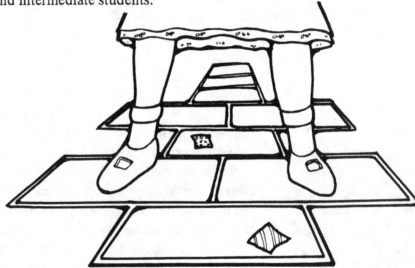

How Two-Feather Was Saved from Loneliness: An Abenaki Legend. C. J. Taylor. Tundra Books, 1990. 17 pages. (0-88776-282-4)

In simple but compelling words, Native American painter C. J. Taylor has retold a legend unique for its breadth: "What is unusual about this Abenaki tale is that it combines three origins into one legend and makes them inseparable: the origin of fire, the origin of corn and the origin of communal life." The story is set in the distant past when "the earth was a cold and lonely place. No one knew how to make fire. There were very few people and they wandered far in search of food." Among these lonely wanderers was Two-Feather. Early one spring, famished from a winter diet of bark and roots, he takes refuge in sleep. Soon he is awakened by a mysterious voice, which he finally determines is coming from the mouth of a strange but very beautiful woman. Instantly enamored, Two-Feather asks the woman to be his. She neither accepts or rejects his overtures but instead tells him that she has come to look after him and asks that he follow her. Eventually they come to a meadow where she teaches him how to make fire and use it to clear away the grasses. Then she insists that Two-Feather grab her long silky hair and drag her across the ground. Before long she has disintegrated into nothing, leaving behind a field sprouting corn stalks. In this way the Corn Goddess gave both fire and corn to humans, which allowed them to take up farming in place of their lonely lives of wandering. The opulent colors of Taylor's paintings will draw students into this multi-faceted legend.

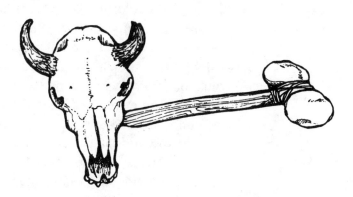

Iktomi and the Buffalo Skull. Paul Goble. Orchard Books, 1991. 28 pages. (0-531-05911-1)

Belonging to Native American oral tradition, this tale, in more than one version, was told throughout most of North America, its sources "among the oldest and most reliable, recorded by ethnologists and anthropologists during the first decade of this century." With italicized asides meant to illicit audience response in the form of laughter and witticisms, Goble's humorous version of Iktomi's exploits fairly begs to be read aloud. Even the captions to the clever illustrations are sure to produce some giggles, recording as they do the egomaniacal thoughts of the silly trickster who, even though he is a married man, decides to gussy himself all up and ride over to the next village to flirt with the girls. But Iktomi never reaches his destination. Instead, after having been deservedly bucked off his horse, he foolishly and irreverently sticks his head inside a sacred buffalo skull to spy on the festivities going on inside, only to have his hair gnawed off by the Mouse People who are conducting a pow wow there. Unable to pull his head back out of the skull, Iktomi resorts to floating down river to camp where his exasperated wife gladly administers some forceful whacks to the skull with a stone hammer, finally cracking it off and leaving her philandering husband one sore-headed man. This delightful story will expose students to a lighter side of Native American culture and develop their listening skills in the bargain.

In the Year of the Boar and Jackie Robinson. Bette Bao Lord.

See page 107 for entry.

Journey to America. Sonia Levitin.

See page 110 for entry.

Kanu of Kathmandu: A Journey in Nepal.
Barbara A. Margolies.
Four Winds Press, 1992.
37 pages. (0-02-762282-7)

While travelling in Nepal, the author met eight-year-old Kanu Sengupta, a resident of Kathmandu, the capital city. The son of the general manager of Kathmandu's Hotel Shangri-la, Kanu had the opportunity to accompany his father and some guests on a tour of the towns and villages on the outskirts of the capital. With her camera, Margolies has recorded the interesting sights they encountered. With her pen, she took down Kanu's reactions to these points of interest as he played the role of tour guide. The result is a charming "travelogue," written from a child's perspective. Full of Margolies's colorful photographs and Kanu's lively observations, this book presents plenty of information in a form palatable to young readers: "See those grass huts on top of poles? Sometimes a farmer has to spend the night in the hut so he can chase away animals that come to eat his crops. I would be afraid to stay alone there! Hmm, maybe I won't be a farmer! . . . Look! There are three Buddhist monks. Oh, there is a *scythe*, a holy man, with a snake! Let's get away . . .I am afraid of snakes!" A listing of several dozen words presented in both English and Nepali and several maps add further interest to this exploration of the tiny kingdom of Nepal, home to Mt. Everest and millions of culturally diverse people.

Keepers of the Earth: Native American Stories and Environmental Activities for Children.
Michael J. Caduto and Joseph Bruchac.

See page 31 for entry.

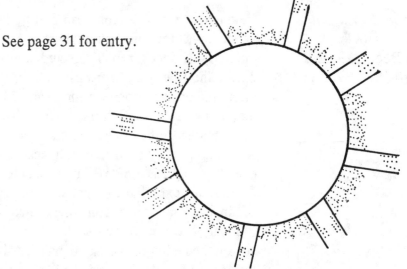

Kenju's Forest. Junko Morimoto. Collins Publishers Australia, 1990. 28 pages. (0-7322-7358-7)

Intoxicated by the beauty of the Japanese countryside as he wanders alone among the rice fields, young Kenju embraces the sky and exultantly laughs aloud, the sight of which produces derisive laughter from the village folk. Undaunted, Kenju continues his love affair with the natural world by planting one of his father's empty fields with hundreds of cedar tree seedlings, tending them faithfully for many years despite the wrath of a neighboring farmer who demands the trees be cut down. One day a large group of children comes to dance and sing among the cedars while Kenju watches from afar filled with a joy that "burst[s] out and melt[s] into the trees." The next winter Kenju dies during an epidemic, but his forest lives on, bringing pleasure to the local children for decades to come, long after the village has become an industrialized town. Morimoto's illustrations effectively convey the expansiveness of both the rural landscape and Kenju's dream-come-true. This is a book that will inspire students of all ages and backgrounds to pursue their dreams with hard work and determination.

The Kingdom by the Sea. Robert Westall.

See page 112 for entry.

Klara's New World. Jeanette Winter. Knopf, 1992. 38 pages. (0-679-80626-1)

With starvation knocking at the door, Klara's parents have decided to escape the poor soil and drought of Sweden and head for Minnesota. Though saddened by the thought of leaving behind her grandfather, Klara understands the necessity of seeking a new life in America: "Our old cow stopped giving milk. We slaughtered our last pig. Mama was running out of flour to bake bread. If our luck didn't change, I knew I would be hired out to rock babies' cradles and tend geese and pigs on the big manor farm, though I was not yet eight years old." Klara and her family endure a miserable ocean voyage to New York during which a number of the passengers succumb to a fever. The victims include an eight-month-old baby who is buried at sea in a tiny coffin made by the ship's carpenter. But all is not gloomy. Klara recovers from her bout with the fever, makes friends among the passengers, and has fun singing and dancing to Old Gustaf's fiddle music. When they finally arrive in Minnesota, Klara and her parents are welcomed by their fellow countryman Bertil and his wife Anna. Bertil helps Klara's father pick out a prime fifty acres and build a one-room cabin on it. Klara is especially thrilled by the sprouting of the blue gentian seeds her grandfather had given her to plant in America. The author's note following Klara's first person narrative supplies historical background regarding the thousands of Scandinavians, who like Klara, made their way to the U.S. during the second half of the nineteenth century. Students will admire Winter's distinctive, intensely colorful depictions of Klara's adventures.

Korea. Karen Jacobsen. Childrens Press, 1989. 48 pages. (0-516-41174-8)

The geography, history, and culture of Korea are presented in a small, light-weight paperback easier for young hands to carry than an encyclopedia volume or a typical hardcover social studies text. Printed in large type on high gloss paper and full of colorful photographs, this book would make an ideal reference source for individual or group projects focused on world cultures. Illustrative of the highly readable prose found in each of its twelve very short chapters are the optimistic closing lines of chapter twelve, "Korea Today": "North Korea would not compete in the Olympics. But, just before the games, there were meetings between North and South. Maybe there will be more meetings. Many Koreans hope that the two parts of Korea can find a way to stop being enemies. Then, real peace will come to the Land of the Morning Calm." Preceding chapters provide basic facts about Korea's beautiful physical features; mild climate; many wars — the Korean War, in particular — status as a divided nation; and outstanding accomplishments in the arts, printing, industry, and education. A list of "Words You Should Know" and a short index conclude this handsome little book.

Kwanzaa. A. P. Porter. Illustrated by Janice Lee Porter. Carolrhoda Books, 1991. 56 pages. (0-87614-545-4)

"For two hundred years, most African Americans were slaves. Slaves in America became free in 1863. The law said freed slaves could do whatever they wanted, but black Americans did not have the same rights as other Americans. . . . At Kwanzaa time, African Americans think about their people, their struggles, and their future." In candid, direct language such as this, Porter provides the historical background that lead Dr. Maulana Karenga to found Kwanzaa, the seven-day holiday that is celebrated each year from December 26 to January 1. Porter then carefully describes the seven symbols of Kwanzaa — a place mat, a cup, fruits and vegetables, candles and a candle holder, corn, gifts, and a flag — and explains the importance of the seven principles that underlie the celebration, principles such as unity, self-determination, cooperation, economic cohesiveness, purpose, creativity, and faith. Each of these symbols and principles is identified by a Swahili word, which is defined in a list of "New Words" that begins the text. Also helpful is a concluding page that provides a concise list of the materials that are needed to celebrate Kwanzaa, but as Porter reminds his readers, "the gifts and symbols of Kwanzaa don't need to cost a lot of money. The ideas matter, not the things." Handsomely illustrated, this book provides numerous facts that would interest anyone unfamiliar with the youthful holiday Kwanzaa.

The Lady of Guadalupe. Tomie de Paola.

See page 112 for entry.

The Land and People of Pakistan. Mark Weston.

See page 114 for entry.

Leaving for America. Roslyn Bresnick-Perry. Illustrated by Mira Reisberg. Children's Book Press, 1992. 32 pages. (0-89239-105-7)

Bresnick-Perry opens her autobiographical work with background that prepares the reader to appreciate her story: "I was born in a shtetl, a little Jewish town in Russia, many years ago. Times were hard for the Jews there, and when I was six months old my father left for America to make a better life for our family. . . . I spent the first seven years of my life with my mother in our little town of Wysokie, without my father. Sometimes I would cry because my father was so far away, but he sent us letters and money and pictures of himself and that made me feel better. This story is about my memories of those years, and of my last days before leaving for America." Bresnick-Perry's story is notable for its colorful detail and subtle mingling of pathos and humor. These qualities appear, for instance, when she describes the final farewell scene. She recalls that of all her relatives, she was crying loudest. To assuage her misery, her grandmother brought some rye bread with chopped liver on it. Bresnick-Perry explains, "I ate my chopped liver crying with much less emotion. After all, how emotional can you be while eating chopped liver?" Here is a book that contains many of the elements common to other immigrant stories but which is far from generic, a fact that Reisbery's distinctive, mixed media art work helps ensure.

72

The Legend of the Bluebonnet: An Old Tale of Texas. Retold and illustrated by Tomie dePaola.

See page 32 for entry.

Legends of Earth, Air, Fire, and Water. Eric and Tessa Hadley. Illustrated by Bryna Waldman. Cambridge University Press, 1988. 29 pages. (0-521-26311-5)

This assortment of myths highlights a trait common to all cultures: the attempt to explain natural phenomena by means of story telling. The traditional stories retold here originated in societies as diverse as Polynesian, Italian, Bantu, Iroquois, Chinese, Aboriginal, Finnish, Cree, Cameroon, and Japanese. They are arranged in four groups corresponding to the four elements — earth, air, fire, and water. Each of these groups contains three myths imaginatively illustrated with Waldman's graceful watercolors. An introductory essay will help arouse students' curiosity in the subject matter, which may seem distant to youngsters of today growing up in urban areas: "When you have read these stories it might be interesting to read them to someone else, and then ask them [sic] to guess where the story-tellers come from. . . . Most of you reading these stories will live in cities or towns. There the earth is buried deep underneath roads and pavement. [But] sometimes it might show itself round the edges of a lawn, or carefully planted and fenced in a park." This collection ends with a unifying "Story of Stories," a Seneca Indian tale that demonstrates the importance of story telling in the passing on of knowledge. Teachers will find that this book can enrich lessons in science and social studies as well as prompt students to create their own myths, which they can "pass on" both orally and in writing.

Let's Celebrate!: Canada's Special Days. Caroline Parry.

See page 115 for entry.

Life in the Polar Lands: Animals, People, Plants. Monica Byles. Scholastic, 1990. 32 pages. (0-590-46130-3)

Though much of this book deals with the physical geography and wildlife of the Arctic and Antarctic regions, some interesting material is provided that pertains specifically to the Inuit, the native people of northern North America and the former USSR. And certainly to understand the Inuit culture, students first need to know something about the extremely beautiful but challenging environment in which this culture evolved. For example, if they have learned that no trees grow within approximately 1,500 miles of the North Pole and that the only existing plant life consists of scrubby tundra growth, students will not be surprised to discover that the traditional Inuit diet is composed of meat and fish only. Likewise, they will better be able to appreciate the Inuit folktale "Crow Steals Some Daylight" after they have contemplated photographs of vast expanses of snow and ice and thus have some comprehension of the fact that heat and light are precious commodities in the Inuit world. Dramatic photographs, attractive drawings, a glossary, a short post-reading true or false quiz, and an index all add to the worth of this book as an introduction to a part of the world that remains an enigma to many.

Little Brother. Allan Baillie.

See page 116 for entry.

Lon Po Po: A Red-Riding Hood Story from China. Ed Young. Philomel Books, 1989. 30 pages. (0-399-21619-7)

Like the European *Little Red Riding Hood*, this ancient Chinese folktale presents evil embodied in the form of a wolf masquerading as a kindly grandma. But unlike its European counterpart, this tale boasts three female protagonists — Shang, Tao, and Paotze — who, without the aid of a male rescuer, defeat the canine villain themselves. Left home alone when their mother sets off to visit their grandmother on her birthday, the three sisters are surprised late that evening to hear someone knock at their door, claiming in a gruff voice to be dear Po Po (Chinese for grandmother). Despite their suspicions, the girls admit the wolf and are duped into letting him climb into bed with them. When Shang finally realizes what a mistake they have made, she sweet-talks the wolf into letting the girls climb up a nearby gingko tree to fetch him some tender nuts. Finally they dash the wolf to pieces by letting go of the rope tied to a basket they have employed in their pretended efforts to hoist the wolf to the top of the tree. Students will have fun comparing the familiar European folktale with this beautifully illustrated Caldecott Medal-winning version of *Lon Po Po*. Older students may want to speculate as to why two such similar stories have evolved as part of the oral tradition of two distinct cultures.

Look What We've Brought You from Mexico: Crafts, Games, Recipes, Stories, and Other Cultural Activities from Mexican-Americans. Phyllis Shalant.

See page 116 for entry.

Lupita Mañana. Patricia Beatty.

See page 117 for entry.

Mary McLean and the St. Patrick's Day Parade. Steven Kroll. Illustrated by Michael Dooling. Scholastic, 1991. 29 pages. (0-590-43702-X)

In 1849 Mary McLean and her family leave behind their thatched hut in Donegal, Ireland. Surviving eight weeks of storms and meager rations, they arrive at Manhattan Island and settle in a cold, cramped room on James Street where many Irish have taken refuge from the Great Potato Famine. Soon the McLeans have fallen into the rhythm of their new lives in America: Mary's dad labors at the docks, her mother works as a maid at a Fifth Avenue mansion, brother Danny sells newspapers, baby Meghan spends her days with Mrs. O'Reilly next door, and Mary attends school. But Mary's aspirations are directed towards things Irish rather than American. When she hears about the St. Patrick's Day parade, she immediately decides that more than anything else she wants to ride in it with Mr. Finnegan the grocer. Each year dressed in a green cloak and driving a gold and green trimmed cart pulled by two white horses, he is the star attraction. Mary boldly makes her desire known to Mr. Finnegan, who says he will allow her to join him and his dog Fergus in the cart IF she brings him a perfect shamrock. After months of trying to locate a shamrock beneath the snow, Mary thinks her only hope lies in catching the wily leprechaun she encountered one day in the park and convincing him to give her the shamrock he wears in his lapel. But in the end it is her father who helps Mary realize her dream. A mixture of realism and fantasy, this story provides a pleasing medium for teaching Irish American history and culture. Large, radiant paintings and an "Author's Note" that supplies facts about the potato blight and St. Patrick will enhance the reading experience of both teachers and students.

Mary of Mile 18. Ann Blades. Tundra Books, 1984. 37 pages. (0-88776-059-7)

Billed as the Canadian Association of Children's Librarians Book of the Year for 1972, a long-standing best-seller, and a Canadian classic, this is one book that lives up to the hyperbole of its cover blurbs. Set in the British Columbia Mennonite community of Mile 18, "a real place, even though it is too small to appear on the map of Canada," this story reveals the stern beauty of life on the edges of the Canadian wilderness. Here Mary Fehr and her family must endure freezing temperatures six months of the year, survive without modern plumbing or electricity, and work hard every day just to subsist. But, at the same time, they are able to enjoy nature's treasures — the glory of northern lights and wide open land that will be deeded to them by the government once they have cleared and planted it. And, most important, the Fehrs share a closeness that comes from the necessity of joining forces daily just to eke out a living. So challenging is the Fehrs' struggle to establish themselves in this harsh environment that Mr. Fehr has set the rule that the children can own no animal unless it can either work or provide them with food. Thus when Mary finds an adorable wolf pup and asks to keep it, Mr. Fehr instructs her to abandon it in the woods. When the persistent little creature shows up again, Mr. Fehr angrily tells Mary to do a better job of getting rid of it. Mary is heart-broken and retreats to her bed without dinner. All turns out happily, however, when the pup later alerts the family to the presence of a coyote that has come to rob the chicken house. Having proved he can earn his keep, the pup ends up in the arms of an overjoyed Mary. Paintings and text alike will warm the hearts of students while exposing them to one facet of Canadian culture.

The Most Beautiful Place in the World. Ann Cameron.

See page 118 for entry.

Mother Goose on the Rio Grande. Francis Alexander.

See page 34 for entry.

Mrs. Katz and Tush. Patricia Polacco.

See page 35 for entry.

Mufaro's Beautiful Daughters: An African Tale. John Steptoe. Scholastic, 1987. 29 pages. (0-590-42058-5)

In a brief introductory statement, author John Steptoe acknowledges his sources: *"Mufaro's Beautiful Daughters* was inspired by a folktale . . . published in 1895. . . in *Kaffir Folktales*. Details of the illustrations were inspired by the ruins of an ancient city found in Zimbabwe, and the flora and fauna of that region. The names of the characters are from the Shona language." From this melange, Steptoe has produced a book of great visual appeal containing an entertaining fairy tale set "a long time ago, in a certain place in Africa." The story involves two beautiful sisters — Manyara, who is notoriously bad-tempered and Nyasha, who is unusually kind. The sisters become rivals as they vie to marry the king, but in the end, Nyasha triumphs, for she, unlike Manyara, has treated the king generously and graciously even when he appeared to her disguised in his various incarnations as a snake, a hungry boy, and an old woman. Dedicated to the children of South Africa, this Caldecott Honor Book will help dispel any residue of the stereotypical images American students may still harbor regarding the appearance and behavior of Africans in pre-colonial times.

Musical Games for Children of All Ages. Esther L. Nelson.

See page 35 for entry.

My Name Is Paula Popowich! Monica Hughes.

See page 119 for entry.

My Place. Nadia Wheatley and Donna Rawlins.

See page 120 for entry.

Native American Doctor: The Story of Susan LaFlesche Picotte. Jeri Ferris.

See page 121 for entry.

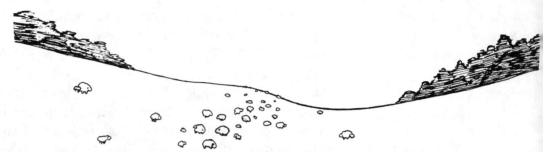

New Zealand. Ronda Armitage. Photography by Chris Fairclough. Illustrated by Stefan Chabluk. Bookwright Press, 1988. 48 pages. (0-531-18158-8)

This information-packed volume contains all the detail necessary for a comprehensive introduction to the island nation of New Zealand. Loaded with multicolored maps, tables, drawings, and photographs, no unadorned page of print exists. These abundant "extras" will draw students into the easy-to-read text, which is divided into seventeen compact "chapters," a glossary, a list of recommended books, and an index. The chapters focus on New Zealand's geographical and political relationship to the rest of the world, its land and climate, wildlife, history, population mix, cities, family life, education, shopping and food, sports and leisure, religion, culture and art, farming and fishing, industry, transportation, government, and future prospects. Conveniently organized to meet the needs of beginning researchers, this attractive volume is tailor made for investigations leading to oral or written reports.

Next-Door Neighbors. Sarah Ellis.

See page 121 for entry.

Night on Neighborhood Street. Eloise Greenfield.

See page 36 for entry.

Now Is Your Time! The African-American Struggle for Freedom. Walter Dean Myers.

See page 122 for entry.

On the Pampas. María Cristina Brusca. Henry Holt, 1991. 29 pages. (0-8050-1548-5)

A memoir recalling a special summer the author spent as child on her grandparents' cattle ranch, this well-written narrative will give students a look at life on the Argentine pampas, "the very flat, almost treeless grasslands that stretch for hundreds of miles through central Argentina and Uruguay." During her stay at the estancia — a large South American cattle ranch — María Cristina spent much of her time with her cousin Susanita trying to master the skills of the gaucho. With the help of Susanita and a gaucho named Salguero, by the end of the summer María Cristina became a competent little rider, roper, and herder. So impressed with her accomplishments were her grandparents that they presented her with a gaucho belt decorated with silver coins from around the world — just like

Salguero's. They also promised her that next summer she would have her very own horse. All of María Cristina's time was not spent on ranch work; she also enjoyed making the two hour ride to the general store where she and Susanita would buy orange sodas and dream of one day owning some of the fancy saddles sold there. She also had fun going hunting for ñandú eggs — eggs of the South American ostrich that are so large she and Susanita needed just one to bake a three-layer birthday cake for their grandmother. Bursca's animated watercolors bring her memories clearly before the readers' eyes and are surely responsible, at least in part, for this work having received the 1991 Parents' Choice Award and its being designated A Notable 1991 Children's Trade Book in the Field of Social Studies.

One Day in the Tropical Rainforest. Jean Craighead George.

See page 122 for entry.

One More River to Cross: The Stories of Twelve Black Americans. Jim Haskins.

See page 123 for entry.

The Pacific Islanders. Douglas Ford.

See page 124 for entry.

Panther Dream: A Story of the African Rainforest. Bob and Wendy Weir. Hyperion Books, 1991. 40 pages. (1-56282-076-1)

Lokuli lives in a small African farming village that is surrounded by rainforest. Though his grandmother is a Pygmy who grew up in the forest, Lokuli has always been warned that he must never go there because of evil spirits. But when the people of his village are running out of meat, Lokuli decides he will go into the forest by himself to hunt. While on this expedition, he encounters a wide variety of plants and animals, including a panther who gives Lokuli an important message: "I see that you are young and do not know the ways of the forest. . . . Respect all life within it. If you need meat, take only enough to live. Then life can continue." With the help of a Pygmy, Lokuli eventually finds his way back home and presents the villagers with some meat and honey. Lokuli's father tries to thank him, but the boy modestly replies, "I did not do this. . . . These are gifts from the rainforest. The forest is not full of evil spirits as you say. It is our friend." Following this conservation-minded story are maps on which the rainforests of the world have been indicated, a key to the book's graceful illustrations, and a glossary providing facts about the plant and animal life of the rainforest. Sold along with this book is an audio tape produced, narrated, and performed by coauthor Bob Weir, guitarist for the Grateful Dead.

People. Peter Spier. Doubleday, 1980. 44 pages. (0-385-13181-X)

Readers of all ages are sure to be fascinated by Spier's copiously illustrated celebration of physiological and cultural diversity: "Imagine how dreadfully dull this world of ours would be if everybody [were to] look, think, eat, dress, and act the same!" Between oversized 10" by 13" covers are colorful depictions of fifteen eye-types; fifty-six nose shapes; twenty-four games, from Japanese thumb wrestling to American horseshoe pitching; twenty-five residential architectures; oodles of pets, feasts, cuisines, holidays, and occupations; writing in twenty-four varied scripts; gods and goddesses galore; and much more. Far from saccharine, the brief but appropriate text treats the human condition honestly: "What is considered beautiful or handsome in one place is considered ugly, and even ridiculous, elsewhere," "some of us excel at things others could never do," and "most people are decent, honest, friendly, and well meaning, but some are none of these." Though Spier might have given more attention to the contributions of women, his winner of the 1980 Christopher Medal and the 1980 National Conference of Christians and Jews National Mass Media Award will provide teachers with a wide array of themes around which to build units that will develop their students' multicultural perspectives.

The People Could Fly: American Black Folktales. Retold by Virginia Hamilton.

See page 38 for entry.

Rose Blanche. Roberto Innocenti and Christophe Gallaz.

See page 126 for entry.

Rechenka's Eggs. Patricia Polacco. Philomel Books, 1988. 30 pages. (0-399-21501-8)

"Babushka lived alone in a *dacha*, a little house in the country, but she was known far and wide for the fine eggs that she lovingly painted. Her eggs were so beautiful that she always won first prize at the Easter Festival in Moskva." More than just a talented artist, old Babushka soon shows herself to be a generous, kindly woman who loves animals. One day when she is feeding the starving caribou outside her door, an injured goose lands at her feet. She immediately carries the bird into her house, places it in her best egg basket lined with her warmest quilt, and proceeds to nurse it back to health. Before long Babushka and the goose, whom she names Rechenka, have become fast friends. As Rechenka gains back her strength, she begins to waddle around Babushka's work area, and disaster of disasters, the goose knocks over the basket containing the old woman's finished eggs.

Babushka resigns herself to the fact she will never be able to complete more eggs in time for the Easter festival, but then a miracle occurs — Rechenka begins to lay eggs even more beautiful than the ones she destroyed! And from the most miraculous egg of all, a gosling hatches to become Babushka's life-long friend when Rechenka is well enough to return to the wild. After reading this heart-warming story full of colorful drawings, students will be eager to try making some Ukrainian eggs, just like the ones Rechenka laid for old Babushka.

Roberto Clemente: Baseball Superstar. Carol Greene. Childrens Press, 1991. 48 pages. (0-516-44222-8)

Young baseball fans will love this easy-to-read biography of baseball great Roberto Clemente. The black Spanish-speaking native of Puerto Rico was not only an outstanding athlete but also a humanitarian who lost his life in a plane crash while en route to Nicaragua to bring supplies to victims devastated by a strong earthquake in 1972. Students will be impressed by Clemente's generosity as well as his achievements on the playing field where he racked up some very impressive statistics: a lifetime batting average of .317, four National League batting titles, twelve Golden Glove awards for fielding, and three thousand hits. The author conveys all this information and more in five brief chapters made up of short free verse stanzas:

> *Many boys on the island*
> *of Puerto Rico*
> *loved baseball.*
> *But Roberto loved it*
> *so much, he would*
> *rather play than eat.*

Students would enjoy using this book as a source on which to base oral presentations or written reports featuring multicultural heros. A map of the Caribbean, a table of important dates, and a brief index are tailor made to assist students with such projects. Also worthy of mention are the numerous black and white photos taken during various stages of Clemente's career.

Sachiko Means Happiness. Kimiko Sakai. Illustrated by Tomie Arai. Children's Book Press, 1990. 32 pages. (0-89239-065-4)

Lately Sachiko has grown to dread sunsets, despite their beauty, because they harbinger the time of day when she must interact with her grandmother. Once beloved, the grandmother now alienates and frustrates Sachiko with behavior indicative of Alzheimer's disease. One evening, feeling tired and deeply hurt over her grandmother's failure to recognize her, Sachiko mischievously encourages the old woman's delusion that she is a little girl who must hurry home to her mother. The grandmother wanders out onto the sidewalk, trying to find her way and soon breaks into tears of confused fright. When Sachiko sees her grandmother crying just like a five-year-old, she realizes for the first time the reality of the situation: " 'It must be very hard,' I thought, 'to suddenly discover that everyone is a stranger to you.' I blinked back tears, but they were not tears of anger." This realistic and moving story told in Sachiko's own words is enhanced by Arai's richly toned drawings that include decorative panels of Japanese floral patterns. Discussions of the love and understanding that one generation can bestow upon another will follow naturally from this treatment of a universally important subject.

Sadako and the Thousand Paper Cranes. Eleanor Coerr.

See page 127 for entry.

The Sailor Who Captured the Sea: The Story of the Book of Kells. Deborah Nourse Lattimore. HarperCollins, 1991. 32 pages. (0-06-023710-4)

"The Book of Kells [now on display at Trinity College in Dublin] is a manuscript of about 340 pages of parchment, richly illustrated with scenes from the Bible. For nearly one hundred years, the monks at the monastery in the Irish city of Kells worked to complete it. . . . Why was it so important? What drove them to pursue their goal. . . ?" In response to these questions which she poses in the prologue, Lattimore has written a short work of fiction telling the story of three brothers — Fursa, Niall, and Broghan — who flee Dublin in the wake of Viking invasions to seek refuge at the monastery of St. Columba located in Kells. Though none of the brothers is trained as an artist, eventually each teaches himself to draw and contributes to the task of finishing the manuscript. Even Broghan, an inveterate sailor unable to believe he possesses any artist abilities, transforms his love of the sea into an inspiration that allows him to develop his own distinctive drawing style. And why, according to Lattimore's imaginative speculations, were these brothers and the monks of St. Columba willing to devote themselves to completing the Book of Kells? They believed that once finished, this remarkable work would protect the monastery from the threat of Vikings and Irish Kings looking to replenish their coffers with monastic treasures. Both the text and Lattimore's gorgeous art work will transport students back in time to early ninth century Ireland where they will gain entrance to the scriptorium, the room in which the monks labored over their literary creations.

Sami and the Time of Troubles. Florence Parry Heide and Judith Heide Gilliland. Illustrated by Ted Lewin. Clarion Books, 1992. 32 pages. (0-395-55964-2)

Set in modern-day Beirut, Lebanon, this simple, beautifully told story captures both the resignation and the hope that colors the lives of children who have grown up amid civil strife. Sami, the young narrator who lost his father to a terrorist bomb, speaks matter of factly about the horror his present life: "I live in the time of the troubles. It is a time of guns and bombs. It is a time that has lasted all my life, and I am ten years old. Sometimes, like now, we all live in the basement of my uncle's house. Other times, when there is no fighting, when there are no guns, we can be upstairs." With the encouragement of his grandfather, who tells funny stories and reminisces about glorious sunsets even as Sami and his family are huddled in the basement listening to the sound of gunfire, Sami is able to hold onto comforting memories and look to the future: "I listen to my sister's soft song, a song my father used to sing, and I think of my father's peach trees. I remember his telling me of his trees many times, the trees of his orchards. I try to think of them now. I try to pretend I am my father walking up the winding road, climbing up and up through the foothills, coming upon his orchards. . . . I wonder if those trees are still there. I wonder if I will ever see them." The story ends with Sami telling of his plans to take part in a children's protest march to end the fighting. With its poetic prose and gorgeous watercolors, this book will enable students to enter Sami's world, empathize with his sorrows, and cherish the blessings of peace.

Samuel's Choice. Richard Berleth. Illustrated by James Watling. Albert Whitman, 1990. 38 pages. (0-8075-7218-7)

In this short work of historical fiction, fourteen-year-old slave Samuel Abraham comes to the aid of General George Washington's troops at the Battle of Long Island. During the months leading up to the outbreak of the Revolution, Samuel has begun to yearn for freedom from his new master Isaac van Ditmas, a strict farmer who underfeeds and overworks his slaves. When Samuel hears talk of Liberty Men and a Declaration of Independence, he ignores the pessimism of friends who say that the battle is not being fought for Africans. He chooses to use his skill as a sailor to rescue American soldiers and soon meets up with Major Gist, becoming his orderly. In this capacity, one stormy night when Washington's army must cross from Brooklyn to Manhattan, Samuel volunteers to feed a guide rope across the water ahead of the army boats. With help of fellow slave Sana, he succeeds, narrowly escaping death in the swirling waters of the East River. Once on land, Samuel learns that van Ditmas has been arrested for assisting the British and ends his narrative by proclaiming his freedom: "From that day forward, we and Isaac's other slaves were to be citizens of a new nation." A map and action-packed illustrations enhance the impact this text will make on students who may be discovering for the first time that heroic African Americans took part in the American War for Independence.

Secret of the Andes. Ann Nolan Clark.

See page 128 for entry.

Shake It to the One That You Love the Best: Play Songs and Lullabies from Black Musical Traditions. Collected and adapted by Cheryl Warren Mattox.

For entry see page 40.

The Skirt. Gary Soto. Illustrated by Eric Velasquez. Delacorte Press, 1992. 74 pages. (0-385-30665-2)

Miata Ramirez finds herself in a predicament that will seem painfully familiar to most students — she has misplaced a treasured possession and is extremely anxious to get it back before her parents discover it is missing. What has she lost? It is the folklórico skirt her mother wore as a child in Hermosillo, Mexico, and recently loaned to Miata for a special occasion. Miata's discomfort over the loss is compounded by two factors. First, she did not obtain her mother's permission before taking the skirt to show it off at school. And second, her parents are expecting to see her wearing it on Sunday when she is scheduled to dance after church. Having lost the skirt on a Friday afternoon, by Saturday morning Miata is desperate and decides to rope her best friend Ana into helping her out. At the library they hatch a scheme, and once their books have been checked out, they head off to the schoolyard where they hope to find the skirt locked inside a bus. After some clever maneuvering and several tense moments, the skirt is retrieved. All ends up happily on Sunday for Miata when she dances, proudly wearing the treasured old skirt under the beautiful new one her mother has just given her as a surprise. Throughout her ordeal, it is clear that Miata is not so much concerned with avoiding parental punishment as she is desirous of pleasing the people she loves. She obviously enjoys a warm relationship with her bilingual parents and has been especially happy since her family moved to the small town of Sanger, California, leaving behind Los Angeles because "her father had gotten tired of the bad air and long commute to his job at an auto-parts store." Full of specific details such as this and snippets of Spanish dialogue, Soto's prose breathes life into the Mexican American characters that people this short novella sprinkled with lively pencil drawings.

The Snow Queen. Hans Christian Andersen.

See page 41 for entry.

Song of Sedna. Robert D. San Souci. Illustrated by Daniel San Souci. Doubleday, 1981. 28 pages. (0-385-24823-7)

The stark beauty of the Far North provides the setting for this adaptation of an Eskimo myth explaining how the beautiful young Sedna is transformed into the goddess of the sea. Full of action and magic, the story follows Sedna from her girlhood home beside the Arctic Ocean to the Island of Birds where she takes up residence with her handsome new husband Mattak. One day Sedna is astonished to find that Mattak is no ordinary human but a bird-spirit disguised in human form. When her father comes by umiak to rescue Sedna, they are pursued across the water by Mattak riding on the back of a fire-breathing sea serpent. Just as the bewinged Mattak is about to swoop down upon them, the cowardly father, attempting to appease the spirits of the sea, casts his daughter into the waves. Aided by seal spirits and a killer whale, Sedna is led through the water to an ice and ivory palace at the bottom of the ocean. To this day, Sedna reigns in the watery realms, granting protection and good fortune to Eskimos seeking her aid. With its dramatic illustrations featuring chilly whites and blues, this National Council for the Social Studies Notable Book will spur students' desire to investigate Inuit culture and broaden their experience with the myth as a universal form of literature.

South America. D. V. Georges. Childrens Press, 1986. 48 pages. (0-516-41296-5)

The geography, history, and cultures of South America are presented in a small, light-weight paperback easier for young hands to carry than an encyclopedia volume or a typical hardcover social studies text. Printed in large type on high gloss paper and full of colorful photographs, this book would make an ideal reference source for individual or group projects focused on world cultures. Illustrative of the highly readable prose found in each of its eight brief chapters is the content of the final chapter, "South America's Future": "The countries of South America have much in common. Most of the people speak Spanish. In Brazil, people speak Portuguese. In most South American countries, the capital cities are centers for industry, banking and trade. There are many modern buildings. Often they stand just blocks from historic sites. But outside the large cities, the way of life is not yet modern. Most people work on farms near small villages. On the smaller farms, few machines are used. Farmers still do much of the work by hand. Change is coming slowly to the villages of South America. To reach and educate people takes a long time, especially in remote places. South America is rich in minerals and oil fields. Its countries are just starting to become modern nations. They have much to look forward to." Several maps, a list of "Words You Should Know," a table showing each country's date of independence and capital city, and a short index round out this handsome little book.

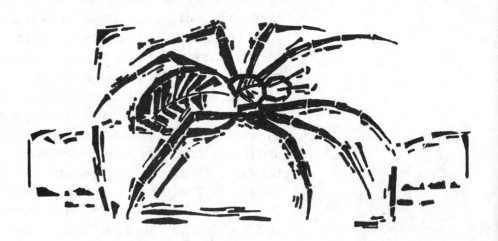

A Story-A Story. Gale E. Haley. Aladdin, 1988. 32 pages. (0-689-71201-4)

"Many African stories, whether or not they are about Kwaku Ananse the 'spider man,' are called 'Spider Stories.' This book is about how that came to be" — so explains the author in the introduction to her retelling of a colorful African folktale featuring the adventures of Ananse in his quest to buy the Sky God Nyame's golden box full of stories. Before this undertaking, the world was devoid of all tales, a situation Ananse decides to remedy by spinning a web up to Nyame's domain and striking a deal with him for the purchase of the stories. Nyame sets a price he is confident the weak old man will be unable to pay, only to discover later that he underestimated Ananse's capabilities; when the clever Ananse succeeds in presenting him with "Osebo the leopard of-the-terrible-teeth, Mmboro the hornet who-stings-like-fire, and Mmoatia the fairy whom-men-never-see," Nyame must allow Ananse to transport the stories to the earth. Haley spices her prose with onomatopoeic African words — "Ananse ran along the jungle path-yiridi, yiridi, yiridi" — and with examples of the repetitive phrasing African storytellers employ for emphasis — "So Ananse tied the leopard by his foot by his foot by his foot by his foot." These features in combination with bright stylized illustrations make this Caldecott Medal recipient a rich source for bringing African culture into the elementary classroom. Students may want to fill a golden box of their own with original Spider Stories modelled after Haley's work.

The Story of George Washington Carver. Eva Moore. Illustrated by Alexander Anderson. Scholastic, 1971. 96 pages. (0-590-42660-5)

The vocabulary and sentence structure of this excellent biography make it readily understandable to intermediate students even as its perceptive, fact-filled discussions of Dr. Carver's personal life and professional achievements could make it an interesting read for much older students. Worthy of special mention is the wonderful job Moore has done in depicting the intensity of the love Carver developed for the natural sciences, botany in particular. Enabling students to imagine the wellspring of this love are passages such as "George spent more and more time taking care of plants. He had a secret garden in the woods where he grew plants and flowers. It was a kind of plant hospital. When George found a dying plant, he would pull it up gently by its roots and plant it in his secret garden. He talked to the plant as he patted dirt around its roots." Moore also has done a commendable job of conveying in simple terms the social conditions that hindered Carver in his quest for an education and in his efforts to improve life for other African Americans. A mixture of black and white photographs and Anderson's attractive drawings contribute much to a work that merits inclusion in every intermediate classroom library.

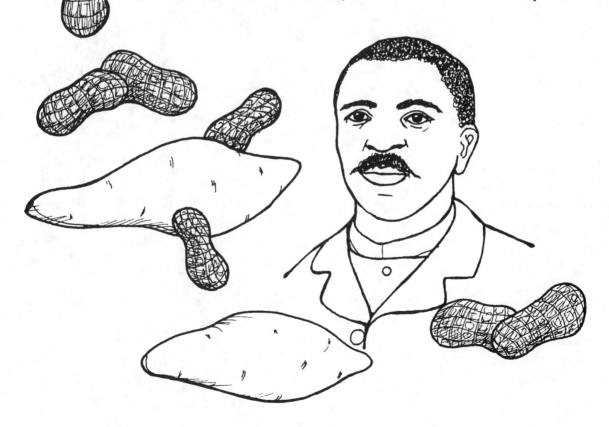

The Talking Eggs: A Folktale from the American South. Retold by Robert D. San Souci. Illustrated by Jerry Pinkney. Dial Books, 1989. 32 pages. (0-8037-0619-7)

Full of local color, San Souci's adaptation of this Creole folktale takes place "back in the old days [when] there was a widow with two daughters named Rose and Blanche. They lived on a farm so poor, it looked like the tail end of bad luck." But Rose and her mother, both "sharp-tongued and always putting on airs," didn't have such a hard time of it, considering they had the sweet, hard-working Blanche to take care of all the work around the place. In the end, however, goodness triumphed; it was Blanche who ended up living in luxury as a result of the kindnesses she showed an old woman she met in the woods. Invited to stay with the woman after she ran away from a particularly severe bout of abuse, Blanche was treated to many amazing sights. She saw a cow with two heads and curly horns, multicolored chickens that whistled like mockingbirds, and rabbits dressed in frock coats dancing and playing the banjo. Through it all, she refrained from reacting impolitely, even when the old woman lifted her head right off her shoulders and set it on her lap to comb and replait her hair. As a reward for her goodness, Blanche was allowed to take home some talking eggs from which emerged wealth of all kinds. Though Rose was given the same opportunities as Blanche, she mistreated the old woman and ended up with eggs that released a plague of wasps and wolves so that she and her mother were forced to "hightail it" to the woods. Award-winning artist, Jerry Pinkney has provided just the right illustrations for this Caldecott Honor Book and Coretta Scott King Award Honor Book whose moral will certainly be obvious to students.

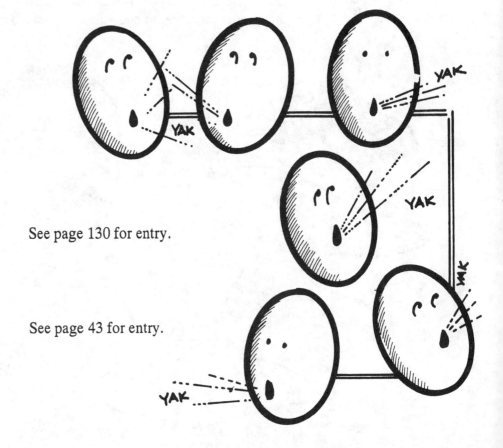

A Thief in the Village and Other Stories. James Berry.

See page 130 for entry.

Thirteen Moons on Turtle's Back: A Native American Year of Moons. Joseph Bruchac and Jonathan London.

See page 43 for entry.

The Turtle and the Island: A Folktale from Papua New Guinea. Retold by Barbara Ker Wilson. Illustrated by Frané Lessac. J. B. Lippincott, 1990. 23 pages. (0-397-32438-3)

The tropical colors of Lessac's paintings help lure the imagination back in time to the primeval waters of the South Pacific where "turtles had teeth, [and] there lived a great sea-turtle, the mother of all sea-turtles, who spent her time swimming about the wide sea." She had no choice; these were the days before the Pacific islands had been created, so the turtle could only dream of resting on a warm beach. One day, however, she came upon a large hill of sand rising from the ocean floor. When she determined that the crest of the hill nearly reached the water's surface, the turtle, bent on realizing her dream, successfully excavated rock and sand and laboriously added it to the hill until an island was born. With the help of birds who dropped seeds, the island became a lush paradise, which the turtle decided to share with the lonely man who lived deep under the ocean in a cave. To satisfy his longing for a mate, she agreed to swim to the mainland and bring him back the beautiful wife he desired. The man and woman soon produced a multitude of children and grandchildren, "and in this way the island became filled with people, who grew crops and built houses and fished along the seashore. And in time the island that the great sea-turtle had made became known as New Guinea." Older students will be able to compare this tale to creation stories from other cultures while students of all ages will be motivated to get out some maps and do some more reading to learn about present-day Papua New Guinea.

Uncle Nacho's Hat/El sombrero del tío nacho. Harriet Rohmer/Rosalma Zubizarreta. Illustrated by Veg Reisberg. Children's Book Press, 1989. 32 pages. (0-89239-043-3)

This adaptation of a Nicaraguan folktale provides a humorous look at a common human foible — the inability to let go of the old and familiar at the expense of change and improvement. In this case, it is Uncle Nacho who has been unable to rid himself of a worthless possession, a tattered old hat that is in desperate need of replacement. Finally one morning when the hat fails to fan the fire back to life, filling the house with smoke, Nacho loses his temper and admits to the hat: "You're useless and full of holes. You're no good for anything anymore!" Nevertheless, even after his niece Ambrosia presents him with a beautiful new hat, Nacho must make many half-hearted attempts before he is finally free of the burdensome old sombrero and able to benefit from accepting the new one. Written in both English and Spanish and illustrated with Reisberg's bold acrylics, this Reading Rainbow Selection has much to offer: English- and Spanish-speaking students will have fun reading together, sharing and comparing each other's languages; bilingual students can employ the dual text in learning to read English; and teachers will find the theme useful in stimulating discussions and writing assignments focused on the benefits of learning to accept and even welcome change.

Under the Sunday Tree.
Eloise Greenfield.

See page 45 for entry.

*We Adopted You,
Benjamin Koo*. Linda
Walvoord Girard.
Illustrated by Linda Shute.
Albert Whitman, 1989. 29
pages. (0-8075-8694-3)

Insightful as well as humorously entertaining, this valuable book depicts the particular challenges faced by students involved with intercultural adoptions. The story is narrated by a fictional nine-year-old named Benjamin Koo Andrews. Benjamin explains that he doesn't know the date of his real birthday or the identity of his real mother because as an infant, he was left on the steps of a Korean orphanage. He has chosen to view his origins in a positive light: "I'll never meet my birthmother, but I know she didn't leave me just anyplace. She left me where she knew loving people could find me easily. I think she really cared about me." Benjamin goes on to describe the affectionate Caucasian American couple who adopted him when he was still a baby. He admits there have been times when he resented the fact that he was being raised by people who are neither his biological parents nor even of the same race. A friendly counselor at school gave him some wise advice that has helped pull him through difficult times: " 'Well,' she said, 'if it walks like a duck and quacks like a duck and acts like a duck, then it *is* a duck. And whoever talks like a mom and loves you like a mom and stands behind you like a mom *is* your mom.' " Benjamin says he has learned to handle other problems such as the words and stares of kids and thoughtless adults who can't seem to accept his race or the fact that his parents don't share it. Adopted students and their classmates have much to learn from the experiences discussed in this appealingly illustrated book.

West Coast Chinese Boy.
Sing Lim.

See page 134 for entry.

When Clay Sings. Byrd
Baylor. Illustrated by Tom
Bahti.   Aladdin, 1972.
27 pages. (0-689-71106-9)

There are/desert hillsides/where/ancient/Indian pottery/still lies/half buried/in the sand/and/lizards/blink at/other dusty lizards/that were painted/on those pots/a thousand years ago." Thus begins Baylor's lyric description of both the varied designs found on pottery crafted long ago in the Southwest and the special connection contemporary Native Americans feel with their ancestral world when they discover a precious clay shard or, better yet, two or three that can be pieced together to reveal an ancient bird or hunter or spirit: "They say/that every piece/of clay/is a piece of someone's/ life./They even say/it has/its own/small voice/and sings in/its own way."   Effectively complementing the text are Tom Bahti's earth-toned renderings of the men, beasts, and geometric patterns gracing the works of the prehistoric Anasazi, Mogollon, Hohokam, and Mimbres cultures that inhabited the Four Corners states of Utah, Colorado, Arizona, and New Mexico. This Caldecott Honor Book and ALA Notable Book, besides delighting the eye and ear, would serve as an excellent introduction to Native American Art as well as a means of peaking the interest of students about to begin more general studies of either Native American culture or the folk art of other peoples.

***When I Was Young in the
Mountains***. Cynthia
Rylant.

See page 46 for entry.

When the Rivers Go Home. Ted Lewin. Macmillan, 1992. 31 pages. (0-02-757382-6)

Lewin's splendid watercolors and spirited prose take readers deep into the heart of Brazil where "there is a marsh the size of Pennsylvania. It's called *Pantanal*, which means 'big swamp' in Portuguese. In the wet season the rivers overflow their banks. . . . In the dry season countless ponds and streams left by the receding water trap millions of fish." It is the dry season — the season during which man and beast converge on the *Pantanal* — that Lewin depicts in this beautiful book. Seeking the abundant fish are countless jacare, alligator-like creatures that clog the waterways. Fortunately for the safety of the many birds such as spoonbills, woodstorks, egret, and herons that frequent the water's edge in search of dinner, the jacare prefer fish to any other delicacy and pose no threat to humans or other animals. Thus the giant rodent, the *capybara*, that loves to wallow in the mud can luxuriate without fear of ending up in the jaws of the fierce-looking jacare. The humans who venture into the swampy land also looking for some good fishing are called the *Pantaneiros*. In their canoes with their fishing poles or bows and arrows, they move unobtrusively among the wildlife. Even the *vaqueiros*, the cowboys who pass along the dirt road that bisects the swampy region, leave nothing behind them but clouds of dust as they and their cattle head for their ranches. This book will demonstrate to students the harmonious relationship that can exist between humans and nature in areas where the resident culture has not yet exploited the land beyond repair. Sadly, Lewin finds it necessary to mention that such harmony will not last for long unless measures are taken to combat the threat posed by outside sources of pollution.

Where the Buffaloes Begin. Olaf Baker.

See page 92 for entry.

Where the Forest Meets the Sea. Jeannie Baker.

See page 47 for entry.

Winter Tales from Poland. Told by Maia Wojciechowska.

See page 136 for entry.

Sixth Through Eighth Grade

All the Colors of the Race.
Arnold Adoff.

See page 7 for entry.

Among the Volcanoes.
Omar S. Castañeda. Dell,
1991. 183 pages.
(0-440-40746-X)

The village of Chuuí Chopaló, located in central Guatemala, is home to Isabel, the oldest daughter of a family with its roots in the ancient Mayan culture. Here Isabel and all the people of her village feel the crush of powerful forces threatening to obliterate their traditional way of life. In the long term, it has been the "ladinos" — descendants of the conquistadors — who have exerted the greatest pressure on the native culture. More recently, the rivalry between Communist guerrillas and government armies has brought repression and murder to Chuuí Chopaló while American tourists and "humanitarians" bring with them their Western ways. Isabel, a bright young woman who aspires to be a teacher, understands these threats to her culture, but at the same time feels a curiosity about the outside world. When her mother's illness does not respond to folk remedies, Isabel is willing to take a daring step, one that horrifies many of her people. She seeks the aid of a young American medical student who has come to Chuuí Chopaló to gather information he hopes will help in the treatment of Mayan-speaking patients. He has tried to enlist the assistance of the villagers, but all have refused to associate with him. Even Isabel suspiciously rebuffs his overtures until the day when her mother's imminent death convinces her to give American medicine a chance. Castañeda's skillfully woven novel ties together the many complex issues facing Isabel and will enrich students' understanding of the cultural clashes that threaten contemporary Guatemalan society.

An Ancient Heritage: The Arab-American Minority. Brent Ashabranner. Photography by Paul S. Conklin. HarperCollins, 1991. 148 pages. (0-06-020048-0)

"Arab Americans form an important ethnic minority in the United States today: about half the size of the Jewish population of the country, for example, and much larger than the total populations of American Indians. Yet of all American ethnic groups of substantial size, Arab Americans probably are the least known and least understood by other Americans." Packed with the names, faces, and stories of individual Arab Americans, Ashabranner and Conklin's well-researched book certainly will help change this situation. Much of the material was gathered during interviews conducted with Arab Americans of various ages and backgrounds. Author and photographer worked as a team to present vivid portraits of Arab Americans such as Hesham Haj Yousif. Hesham, today a law student at American University in Washington, D.C. and a speaker of "flawless English," recalls that life in the U.S. was not always easy for him: " 'The kids pronounced it A-rab,' Hesham said. 'I was a dirty A-rab.' " In contrast, Warren David, a forty-year-old second-generation Arab American who works in financial management, recalls that his parents had no difficulty adjusting to American culture and spoke only English to Warren and his siblings. But as he grew older, Warren found that he wanted to make his Arab heritage an important part of his life: " 'I joined Arab student clubs at the university, became active in Arab student affairs. I decided I wanted to marry a woman from the Arab world.' " Much ignorance and many stereotypes can be dispelled if students are given the opportunity to read and discuss books like this one.

The Arab Americans. Alixa Naff. Chelsea House, 1988. 111 pages. (0-87754-861-7)

As senior consulting editor to the extensive series *The Peoples of North America* of which this book is a part, Senator Daniel Patrick Moynihan has written a fine introductory essay outlining the history of immigration to both the U.S. and Canada and stating the guiding principle behind the series: "The people of North America are the descendants of one of the greatest migrations in history. And that migration is not over. . . . To understand ourselves, we must know something about our diverse ethnic ancestry. Nothing so defines the North American nations as the motto on the Great Seal of the United States: *E Pluribus Unum* — Out of Many, One." This particular book begins with a chapter that clearly defines just what peoples and countries can accurately be described as Arab and provides a concise overview of Arab migration to North America. Succeeding chapters provide more detailed information on Arab culture,

94

the two major migration waves (pre-WWI Christian Syrian influx and post-WWII Muslim flow from a variety of countries), assimilation vs. cultural retention, and contributions made by Arab Americans such as writer Kahlil Gibran, journalist Helen Thomas, diplomat Philip Habib, clothing manufacturer Joseph Haggar, educator Donna Shalala, entertainer Casey Kasem, and consumer activist Ralph Nader. Numerous photographs, including a "Picture Essay" of colored photos depicting present-day Arab American life, round out this instructive work.

Arctic Explorer: The Story of Matthew Henson. Jerri Ferris. Carolrhoda Books, 1989. 80 pages. (0-87614-507-1)

Purely as a piece of adventure writing, this work of nonfiction has much to recommend it. Students will be fascinated by the danger and daring that were involved with early explorations of the regions around the North Pole. But Ferris's book has much more to offer. In bringing the name Matthew Henson before the public eye, it gives an African American hero the recognition he failed to gain, following his courageous assaults on the Pole as a member of Robert Peary's expeditions. Unlike the white Peary who received both the glory and financial rewards one would expect after such accomplishments, Henson was ignored by most and forced to work in obscurity at low wages. "After 1909 [the date of their last, triumphant expedition] Robert Peary was an honored American hero, a retired admiral on a comfortable pension. After 1909 Matthew Henson was a parking garage attendant in Brooklyn for $16 a week." The injustice of this situation will be especially apparent to students after they have read evidence indicating that without the aid of the strong and intelligent Henson, there is a good chance Peary would have never made it to the North Pole, a fact Peary more-or-less admitted to a few associates but purposely kept from the public. Fortunately, towards the end of his life, Henson was finally given some of the attention he deserved. Then in 1988 his body was moved to Arlington National Cemetery and placed next to the grave of Admiral Peary. "The final wrong was made right." Several maps, occasional black and white photographs, and a bibliography listing both primary and secondary sources make this a valuable book for students researching African American role models or the history of racial inequality.

Best-Loved Folktales of the World. Selected and with an introduction by Joanna Cole.

See page 11 for entry.

The Biographical Dictionary of Black Americans. Rachel Kranz. Facts on File, 1992. 190 pages. (0-8160-2324-7)

A resource that certainly belongs in every school library, if not in the bookcase of every upper grade classroom, this work presents information on the lives and achievements of almost two hundred African Americans. Their fields of endeavor include government, the arts, entertainment and athletics, business, education, the law and military, social activism, and the sciences. Each entry, listed alphabetically according to last name, consists of a well-organized essay of several hundred words that begins by outlining significant accomplishments, proceeds with a chronological description of the life, and concludes with bibliographic information on books for further reading. This work is enhanced by occasional black and white portraits and an extensive index that list names of not only the people profiled but also other important African Africans who, because of space limitations, were not included in the text but who students may want to research using other sources.

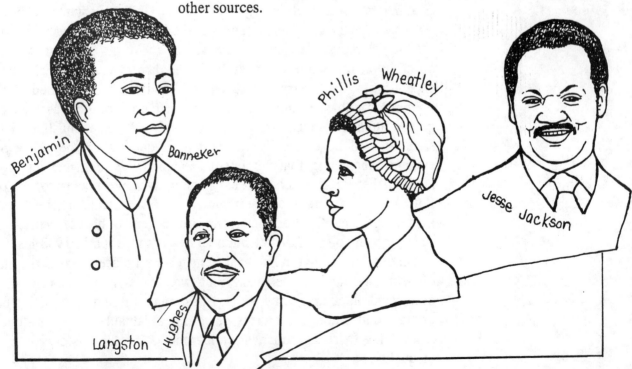

Brother Eagle, Sister Sky: A Message from Chief Seattle. Chief Seattle. Illustrated by Susan Jeffers. Dial Books, 1991. 24 pages. (0-8037-0969-2)

This adaptation of Chief Seattle's famous message captures the dignity and grandeur of the Native American philosophy regarding the sacred relationship between man and nature. Spoken in response to negotiations with the U.S. government over land in the Pacific Northwest, Seattle's words ring as true today as they did 150 years ago and will inspire students to take up the cause of preserving the environment for themselves and future generations: "The earth is our mother. What befalls the earth befalls all the sons and daughters of the earth. . . . What will happen when the buffalo are all slaughtered? The wild horses tamed? What will happen when the secret corners of the forest are heavy with the scent of many men? When the view of the ripe hills is blotted by talking wires? . . . It will be the end of living, and the beginning of survival." Jeffers paintings movingly portray the beauty of the natural world inhabited by Native Americans before the intrusion of European settlers as well as hint at the destruction soon to be wrought by the introduction of practices such as clear-cutting huge forest tracts. A fine primary source for the study of Native American history and culture, this book has much to offer readers from intermediate age through adulthood.

Camels Can Make You Homesick and Other Stories. Nazneen Sadiq.

See page 53 for entry.

The Caribbean: The Land and Its People. Eintou Pearl Springer. Silver Burdett Press, 1988. 45 pages. (0-382-09475-1)

"The Caribbean is an area of cultural diversity and growth. Its culture has evolved through contributions made by the many different peoples living in the region. Each country has its own cultural identity, but there are common regional themes." To understand the rich variety found in the Caribbean today, students need some rather extensive background regarding the flow of peoples into the area — beginning with the arrival of Christopher Columbus — and its impact on the evolution of Caribbean culture. Springer provides just that background and does so by way of sixteen brief chapters that eschew the Eurocentric view of Caribbean history that has often colored the information presented in standard textbooks. Without resorting to hyperbole, Springer explains the influence the ruling Europeans had on the native Amerindians, African slaves, and indentured workers brought in from China, India, and Africa, as well as from other parts of the world. Each of these groups has added distinctive ingredients to the languages, arts, religions, and economies of the more than thirty existing Caribbean countries, many of which are now independent nations. In addition to Springer's lucid prose, this book offers a variety of maps, numerous colored photographs, a detailed listing of important dates and events in Caribbean history, and a thorough index.

The Children of Nepal. Reijo Harkonen.

See page 13 for entry.

Children of Promise: African-American Literature and Art for Young People. Charles Sullivan, ed. Harry N. Abrams, 1991. 126 pages. (0-8109-3170-2)

Both students and teachers will find themselves going back to this book time and time again to explore its varied contents: poems; lyrics; and excerpts from short stories, plays, novels, autobiographies, speeches, documents, and nonfiction books, all of which illuminate the African American experience from colonial times through the present. The large variety of visual art work, usually appearing adjacent to literature with a similar theme, encompasses paintings, sculpture, photographs, and reproductions of documents. The dozens of writers and artists whose work is found in this wonderful collection include, to name but a few, James Baldwin, Gwendolyn Brooks, Frederick Douglass, W. E. B. Du Bois, Mari Evans, Langston Hughes, Abraham Lincoln, Harry S. Truman, Booker T. Washington, Phillis Wheatly, Romare Bearden, Edgar Degas, Winslow Homer, Besty Graves Reyneau, and Augustus Saint-Gaudens. Five pages of biographical notes identify the authors' and artists' life span dates, places of birth, and major accomplishments. This work has limitless potential for stimulating student projects in the language arts, social studies, and visual arts.

Children of the Yukon. Ted Harrison.

See page 14 for entry.

The Children's Jewish Holiday Kitchen. Joan Nathan.

See page 14 for entry.

The Court of the Stone Children. Eleanor Cameron. Puffin Books, 1990. 191 pages. (0-14-034289-3)

An interesting mix of fact and fantasy, this novel opens in modern-day San Francisco where sixteen-year-old Nina is having difficulty adjusting to her new surroundings. Feeling lonely and rather out-of-place, she retreats into the world of a small French museum. The first item that catches Nina's attention is a painting by Chagall entitled *Time Is a River Without Banks*. Nina ponders the meaning of this enigmatic work and before long finds herself caught up in a series of events that involve a strange blending of the past with the present. These mysterious events occur within portions of the museum that have been filled with furnishings taken from a 19th century French estate. Here Nina meets a young girl named Dominique, who lived on the estate during the time of Napoleon. Domi explains that she has ventured into the twentieth century for the purpose of setting the historical record straight regarding her father, the subject of a biography that has just been completed by Helena Staynes, a curator at the museum. The biography records as fact that Dominque's father was guilty of murder, and Domi wants Nina to help bring to light evidence that will clear her father's name. Eventually, Nina finds just the facts she needs to convince Mrs. Staynes that she must revise the biography. Combining bits of historical fact with lots of imaginative fiction, this winner of the National Book Award would make an entertaining addition to a social studies unit covering French history and culture.

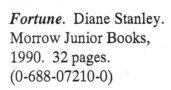

Fortune. Diane Stanley. Morrow Junior Books, 1990. 32 pages. (0-688-07210-0)

The dress, architecture, and social life of "long ago" Persia are beautifully rendered in the illustrations that grace this instructive fairy tale. Set in the "poorest corner" of the country, the story follows Omar, the son of a farmer, who leaves behind Sunny, his betrothed, to seek his fortune. Once he has found a way to earn a living, he fully intends to return to marry Sunny, a loving friend since childhood. He has always appreciated her cheerful disposition, diligence, bright eyes, and delightful laugh and felt undisturbed by her wind-blown hair and soiled work apron. But the situation changes when with the aid of a performing tiger, Omar accumulates enough wealth to build a fine house and spend his days in leisure. Now considering himself much too grand to marry the likes of Sunny, he tells her so and goes off looking for a beautiful princess whom he thinks a man of his affluence must have to be happy. In the end, Omar is deprived of the princess of his dreams when the tiger regains his princely form and marries her. Omar realizes how foolish he was to have rejected Sunny and asks her to marry him. At first, she teasingly refuses but then accepts. While giving students a taste of traditional Persian culture, this story will also prompt them to question how important social class and material wealth are in achieving happiness.

The Friendship. Mildred D. Taylor. Illustrated by Max Ginsburg. Dial Books, 1987. 53 pages. (0-8037-0417-8)

Featuring the same basic cast of characters that appears in Taylor's acclaimed novel *Roll of Thunder, Hear My Cry*, this short story depicts a shocking example of racial violence. The story opens with Cassie Logan and her three brothers in the Wallace store. Their parents have told them to stay clear of the place, but Wallace's is the only store nearby, and they have promised to get Aunt Callie something to ease her terrible headache. The children haven't been in the store long before they get a taste of what their parents hoped they could avoid. The Wallace brothers begin harassing six-year-old Little Man, calling him dirty: "Just look at ya! Skin's black as dirt. Could put seeds on ya and have 'em grown' in no time!" Unfortunately, this is tame if measured against what lies ahead. When old Mr. Tom Bee comes into the store and asks to buy some sardines and candy, the Wallace brothers decide he doesn't really need them and refuse to ring up his purchase. But Tom won't stand for such treatment: "Y'all can't get them sardines and that candy for me, y'all go get y'alls daddy and let him get it! Where John anyway?" The fact that Tom has used their father's first name sends the brothers into a frenzy: "Old nigger, don't you never in this life speak to me that way again. And don't never stand with yo' black face and speak of my daddy or any other white man without the proper respect." Eventually the father appears, and the situation escalates until Tom has been shot in the leg, simply for persisting in calling Wallace by his first name. Illustrated with splendid pencil drawings, this powerful story, winner of the Coretta Scott King Award, is a natural for opening up discussions about racism among students not yet ready for Taylor's longer works.

Games of the World: How to Make Them, How to Play Them, How They Came to Be. Swiss Committee for UNICEF.

See page 25 for entry.

The Girl Who Changed Her Fate: A Retelling of a Greek Folktale. Laura Marshall. Atheneum, 1992. 29 pages. (0-689-31742-5)

Marshall's emotion-filled oil paintings deserve star billing in this retelling of a Greek folktale that explores the ability of humans to change their fate. In the first painting, a worried-looking, middle-aged woman is standing in front of three lovely, sad-faced maidens dressed in traditional Greek attire. According to the text, they are a widow and her three daughters. The girls — though kind, beautiful, intelligent, and desirous of marriage — have never been courted. A wise old crone discovers the source of their troubles and reveals it to the widow: "Ah, it's your youngest who is troubled! She is ill-fated! Each of us has a fate. When a person is born, that fate makes a promise to help and guide one. A good-hearted fate means a happy life! But sometimes a fate forgets her promise and becomes wild and cruel." The crone goes on to explain that the youngest daughter, Eleni, is cursed with an ill-hearted fate and must leave her family to save her sisters from sure spinsterhood. Eleni overhears the old woman's words and immediately insists that she leave home. During her travels she unsuccessfully tangles several times with her fate, embodied in the form of a wild-eyed, raving female entity that is vividly portrayed in Marshall's paintings. Finally, upon the advice of a queen, Eleni journeys to the home of all the fates. After a frightening confrontation with her fate, she succeeds in softening its heart. Younger readers will probably be most interested in Eleni's eery, frightening encounters with the supernatural entity while older, more advanced students will enjoy discussing the concept of fate and may want to do some research into the view of fate held by various Greek philosophers.

Gold! The Klondike Adventure. Delia Ray. E. P. Dutton, 1989. 90 pages. (0-525-67288-5)

Students who think of history books as dry and over-burdened with bloodless fact will be pleasantly surprised when they discover that this work reads more like an exciting adventure story. Ray's prose and numerous fascinating photos capture the excitement of the short-lived but consequential frenzy that followed the discovery of gold in the Yukon Territory: "Although the gold rush of 1898 was amazingly brief, the effects of this event are still evident today.... As if a hidden door had been flung open, the mystery surrounding Alaska and northwest Canada disappeared. Suddenly, the North was a frontier for opportunity." As a result, the natural landscape and population mix of this region changed forever. But Ray does not explore this fact. Instead, she focuses on the dramatic efforts required to reach this mountainous region and then survive its extremes of cold, heat, and lack of material comforts. The effects the influx of gold-hungry Americans and others has had on native Canadians — including the Tagish Indians, two of whom played a central role in the discovery of the Klondike gold — is a subject students may want to explore once Ray's book has provided them with some of the historical background necessary for understanding the social situation in the Yukon of modern-day Canada.

The Grandchildren of the Incas. Ritva Lehtinen and Kari E. Nurmi. Photography by Matti A. Pitkanen. Carolrhoda Books, 1991. 40 pages. (0-87614-566-7)

"The Inca Empire disappeared long ago. But many of the people who now live in and around the Andes Mountains are descendants of the Incas. The people that are most often identified with their Incan ancestors are the Quechua Indians. These are the people we will call 'the grandchildren of the Incas.' " It is the lives of these "grandchildren" as well as the Incas themselves that this fascinating book explores. Pitkanen's gorgeous photographs take the reader right up to the shores of Lake Titicaca to view the modern-day Native American settlements there and high into the Andean jungle to marvel at the ruins of Machu Picchu — the lost city of the Incas — as well as into the streets of Cuzco, the Inca's first settlement and capital city, where Quechua Indians today sell and trade homemade pastries, produce, and clothing made from llama, alpaca, and sheep wool. The many close up portraits of the Quechua introduce the reader not only to their colorful, distinctive dress but to the individuals named and discussed in the fact-filled text, which presents both the astonishing accomplishments and deplorable hardships that have characterized the existence of the Incas and their progeny. A map, pronunciation guide, tables of vital statistics, and an index complete this unique source for teachers wanting to provide their students with the opportunity to investigate the cultures of specific Native *South* Americans.

The Great Deeds of Heroic Women. Retold by Maurice Saxby. Illustrated by Robert Ingpen. Peter Bedrick Books, 1990. 151 pages. (0-87226-348-7)

Award-winning author and authority in the field of children's literature, Maurice Saxby provides an enchanting collection of stories, each of which highlights one of eighteen remarkable "women who stir the imagination because of their courage, intelligence, boldness, forcefulness and strength of purpose. Not all are 'good' women. A few are malevolent. But they all embody aspects of human nature that have existed in all societies through the ages." Some of the women are products of myth and legend while others are historical figures. They include representatives from a variety of cultures: Athena, Aphrodite, Demeter, Atlanta, Circe, and Medea of ancient Greece; Guanyin of ancient China; Rahab, Esther, and Judith from early Jewish tradition; the Queen of Sheba and Scheherazade of ancient Arabia; Boadicea of first century Britain; Joan of Arc of medieval France; Vasilissa of tsarist Russia; Mary Bryant of eighteenth century Britain; and Native Americans Pocahontas and the Zuñi Hunter Maiden. Gracing each of the expertly narrated stories is an arresting portrait by noted artist Robert Ingpen. Along with their indisputable entertainment value, these stories offer a good deal of historical and cultural information that students can explore in greater depth by conducting some independent research.

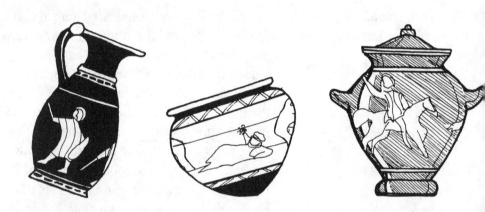

A Greek Potter. Giovanni Caselli. Illustrated by Giuliano Fornari. Peter Bedrick Books, 1986. 30 pages. (0-87226-101-8)

The introduction to this instructive piece of historical fiction nicely prepares students for journeying back in time to meet some ordinary citizens of ancient Greece: "The Greek family in this story lived in Athens during the last half of the fifth century BC. At that time, the city was rich and powerful, and a center for culture and the arts. The story is set in 420 BC, an exciting year. The Olympic Games were held at midsummer, which was the Greek New Year. . . . Pericles, the great Athenian leader, had died of the plague 10 years before in 430 BC, but work was still going on at all the magnificent temples he had ordered to be built. . . . The Athenians were very proud of their artists and crafts men. In this story, Meidias the potter and his family live in the Ceramicus, an area of Athens which lay between the city wall and the Agora, or market place. This was the potters quarters." With this background, the reader is then ready to follow the daily labors of Meidias who — with the aid of his ten-year-old son Apollodorus, several skilled painters, and his many hard-working slaves — has the honor of crafting the splendid pots that will be awarded as prizes to the champions of the Festival Games held to honor Athena, the patron goddess of the city of Athens. Meidias must travel to Phalerum to mine the clay he needs, laboriously prepare the clay, and skillfully shape it on his potter's wheel. Next, he supervises its decoration and firing. Finally, he and his family take part in the activities at the festival and then enjoy a respite from the daily routine by travelling to the countryside to help Meidias's father with the harvest of his olives. Part of "The Everyday Life of . . ." series, this attractively illustrated book succeeds not only in exposing students to various aspects of life in ancient Greece but provides a good deal of information on the potter's craft.

A Hand Full of Stars.
Rafik Schami. Translated by Rika Lesser. Puffin, 1992. 195 pages.
(0-14-036073-5)

The perceptive, often witty journal entries of a Christian Syrian youth comprise this award-winning novel. Begun when the boy was fourteen and spanning three and a half years, the journal depicts both the terror and pleasure of growing up in modern-day Damascus:

> *"October 12--There was another coup today. School will be closed till next Monday. This is the second time schools have closed this year. In Damascus coups like these generally start at dawn. We who live in the old quarter first get wind of what's happening on the radio. Suddenly everything's quiet; then brisk military music comes on, and then the new government's communiqúes. . . ."*

> *"October 25--Autumn is the season I like best. Damascus is at its most beautiful. Swallows fill the sky with their vivid cries, as if anxious to reap the last joys before setting out on their long journey south."*

More than just a series of descriptive passages, the journal entries also propel a lively plot that traces the young author's coming of age as he grapples with the repressive political realities of his environment, explores romance with the daughter of a government spy, and resolves the conflict between his literary aspirations and his father's insistence that he quit school to help with the family bakery. Winner of the Mildred L. Batchelder Award, this ALA Notable Book and ALA Best Book for Young Adults illuminates Arab culture as well as demonstrates the rewards of keeping a personal journal.

Harpoon of the Hunter.
Markoosie. Illustrated by Germaine Arnaktauyok. McGill-Queen's University Press, 1970. 81 pages.
(0-7735-0102-9)

In reading this dramatic novella-length work, students will experience the first piece of Eskimo fiction ever translated into English. Depicting "life in the old days, not as it appeared to southern eyes, but as it has survived in the memory of the Eskimos themselves," the narrative follows the adventures of sixteen-year-old Kamik. As the story opens, Kamik is wondering if he is yet ready to wield his harpoon against the most dangerous prey of all, the bear. Before he has time to pass judgement on himself, he is propelled into action — a rabid bear attacks his camp, mutilating five dogs, and it is decided that the animal must be tracked down and stopped. Eventually, the bear is killed but not before Kamik's father and all his fellow hunters have met the same fate. Afterwards, all alone and far from home, Kamik has the courage to fend off both wild animal attacks and near starvation. But when his mother and wife-to-be are killed while taking part in his rescue, the accumulation of deaths is unbearable, and he decides to take his own life: "Kamik looked at the harpoon in his hands. Now the time had come. Now was the time to find peace, and to find the family and people he loved. He kneeled and put the tip of the harpoon to his throat. Suddenly he pushed it in. And, for the last time, the harpoon of the hunter made its kill." Markoosie's unconventional narrative style and graphic recreation of the challenges Kamik faced will fascinate those students who are emotionally mature enough to accept the harsh reality of traditional Eskimo life.

Hawaii Is a Rainbow. Stephanie Feeney.

See page 26 for entry.

Hello, My Name Is Scrambled Eggs. Jamie Gilson. Pocket Books, 1986. 159 pages. (0-671-67039-5)

What happens when Harvey Trumble, a well-meaning seventh grader from Pittsfield, Illinois, decides to Americanize a newly arrived Vietnamese immigrant? At first, Harvey thinks all is just fun and games. Within a few days, he has Tuan Nguyen eating hot dogs, playing computer games, toilet papering the local park, and spouting slang — "OK," "Shut up!" and Harvey's favorite, "No Kidding!" He even takes it upon himself to change Tuan's name to "Tom Win." Then the reality of the situation begins to sink in. To begin with, Harvey can tell that Tuan doesn't always know what he is actually saying; this becomes embarrassingly apparent when Tuan good-naturedly tells the principal of their middle school to "Shut up!" Harvey also discovers that behind Tuan's polite smiles and calm demeanor resides the pain of having witnessed pirates murder his uncle aboard the fishing boat that was taking his family from Vietnam to Malaysia. On top of this, Tuan suddenly lets Harvey know that he is less than thrilled with his new name. " 'Harvery?' he says, 'I am not Tom. I decide. I will be American. I will. But my name is Tuan Nguyen.' " Harvey accepts that he has been a little overzealous in his attempts to ignore the fact that Tuan is and always will be attached to his Vietnamese heritage. By the end of the story, the two boys are planning to share a Thanksgiving meal together at which both pumpkin pie and *Pho tai* will be on the menu. Full of humor and high jinx, this entertaining novel will promote laughter as well as a greater sensitivity to challenges that new immigrants face.

In the Year of the Boar and Jackie Robinson.
Bette Bao Lord. Illustrated by Marc Simont. Harper & Row, 1984. 169 pages. (0-06-024003-2)

Charming, amusing, irresistible — these and a long list of similar adjectives could accurately be applied to Lord's novel covering the eventful year in the life of ten-year-old Shirley Temple Wong when she leaves behind her tradition-laden existence in the bosom of the House of Wong to emigrate from China to Brooklyn, New York. The winsome Shirley (so named because the only other American name she can think of is "Uncle Sam") confronts the expected challenges with a verve that can't help but impress. On the other hand, the relative ease with which she learns English, makes new friends, and embraces Americanisms such as a passion for baseball all might seem a little too good to be true-to-life to some readers, especially students who may still be struggling with their own immigrant status. Nevertheless, Lord's lively prose style, Simont's delightful drawings, and the entertainment value of this work go a long way in compensating for its possible short-comings. It certainly offers a palatable means of initiating discussions about the ways students might help newly immigrated classmates to become comfortable in an unfamiliar environment.

Indian Chiefs. Russell Freedman. Holiday House, 1987. 151 pages. (0-8234-0625-3)

The white man's treachery in his dealings with the Native Americans he encountered as he pushed his way into the western U.S. is well-documented here as it has been elsewhere, but in this case, the victims have been given names, faces, and personal lives, which makes both their suffering and bravery all the more poignant. A separate chapter is devoted to the biography of each of six remarkable chiefs whose task it was to protect his tribe and its lands during a particularly difficult period: "By the mid-1800s the eastern tribes had been defeated, subdued, and scattered, and the advancing frontier had caught up with the tribes that had always lived in the West. [These] six chiefs. . . were called upon to lead their people at a time of crisis. Each of these men tried to meet that challenge in his own way." Numerous photographs, paintings by Frederic Remington and others, and a well-written text filled with direct quotation will hold students' interest as they develop an understanding of the heroism and hardship that characterized the lives of Red Cloud of the Oglala Sioux, Satanta of the Kiowas, Quanah Parker of the Comanches, Washakie of the Shoshonis, Joseph of the Nez Perces, and Sitting Bull of the Hunkpapa Sioux.

Indian, Soldier, and Settler: Experiences in the Struggle for the American West. Robert M. Utley. Jefferson National Expansion Historical Association, 1990. 84 pages. (0-931056-01-2)

In this slim paperback written for the Jefferson NEHA and the National Park Service, historian Robert Utley attempts to dispel the stereotypes many Americans have formed regarding the Native Americans, frontier soldiers, and settlers who tangled in the West during the nineteenth century. Up until the last several decades, these groups were generally viewed as "grim-faced pioneers in covered wagons trekking westward to carve a civilization out of the wilderness; warriors with feathered bonnets on fleet ponies sweeping down on corralled wagons and circling in attempted massacre; cavalry charging with bugles sounding, banners whipping, and sabers flashing to put Indians to rout and save the day." More recently, these older stereotypes have given way to different but similarly deceptive impressions of "pioneers who were grasping ravaners of the land and oppressors of the native, soldiers who were brutes rampaging about the West taking fiendish delight in slaughtering Indian women and children, Indians ennobled in the mold of James Fenimore Cooper's *The Last of the Mohicans*." By focusing on the lives of actual human beings, Utley has produced a fascinating work that goes a long way in revealing the complex motivations of the ordinary people who played out their lives in the American West. Specifically, Utley provides biographical information on Native American Dewey Horn Cloud, a veteran of Wounded Knew; army bugler William D. Drown, a long-time frontier soldier; and four pioneer women, sisters who were held captive by the Cheyenne. Packed with graphic detail and lots of historical photographs and paintings, this book is sure to engross and enlighten older students.

An Indian Winter. Russell Freedman. Karl Bodmer. Holiday House, 1992. 88 pages. (0-8234-0930-9)

Today on the Fort Berthold Reservation in North Dakota lives a group of Native Americans called the Three Affiliated Tribes. One hundred and fifty years ago, the ancestors of these people lived as three distinct tribes — the Mandans, Hidatsas, and Arikaras. But a small pox epidemic, the slaughter of the buffalo, and the expropriation of lands forced the tribes onto the reservation where they merged, becoming one culture. This book offers the rare chance to look back at the Mandan and Hidatsa cultures before this merging. Drawing on an unusual source — the detailed journals kept by Prince Alexander Philipp Maximillian, a German adventurer and naturalist — Russell Freedman describes the customs of these peoples as they appeared to an educated European observer in the year 1833. Freedman quotes extensively from Maximillian's journals, providing additional information and "corrections" where he sees fit. For instance, when quoting Maximillian's description of a Hidatsa corn dance, Freedman explains that the women dancers were not just "pretending" to be inhabited with the spirits of animals but actually believed in the reality of the spirit world. Adding greatly to the interest of this book is the fact that Maximillian brought with him a young Swiss artist, Karl Bodner, to provide a detailed visual record of his adventures. Happily, Freedman has included many of Bodner's sketches and colorful paintings. Older students will appreciate the unique look into the past that this book offers and may be stimulated to do further reading about the Native Americans of the North Dakota area.

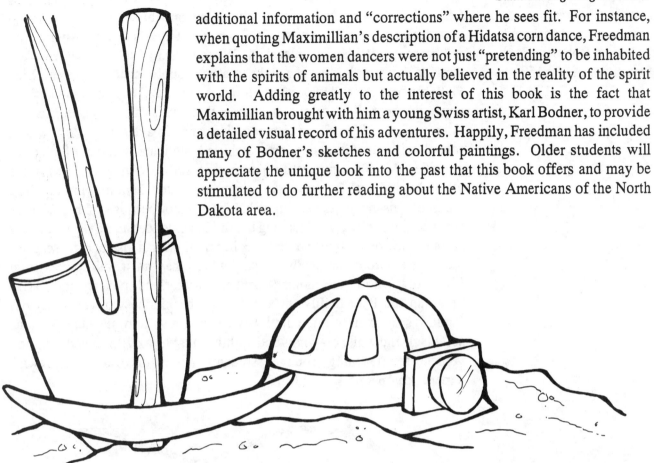

Jonathan Down Under. Patricia Beatty. William Morrow, 1982. 219 pages. (0-688-01467-4)

Living under the harsh conditions of Ballarat, a mid-nineteenth century Australian gold rush camp, thirteen-year-old American Jonathan Cole encounters hunger, gruelling physical labor, illness, betrayal, the death of his father, and the murder of a beloved surrogate mother. But he survives all of it with the help of a motley group of friends. There is Prince Billy, a young aborigine belonging to the Kulin band. Billy takes a special interest in Jonathan when he discovers that Jonathan too is missing his right upper tooth — the tooth ceremonially knocked out by Kulin to signify manhood. Though neither boy ever masters more than a few words of the other's language, they develop a close, mutually beneficial attachment. Jonathan is also befriended by the camp doctor, a Scotsman who saves his eyesight and lends him money and by an Irish woman convict, who nurses him during his bout with trachoma and takes him in after he is orphaned. When this beloved women is murdered, two grizzly-looking male convicts, both of whom Jonathan has long feared and detested, hire him to work on their mining claim and eventually supply him with the means to return to the U.S. Often harrowing but also engrossing, especially during the second half, this novel offers an unromanticized view of the physical environment and the multicultural society found in the mining regions west of Melbourne during a colorful period in Australian history. An interesting seven-page author's note discusses the authenticity of the material used in creating Jonathan's story.

Journey to America.
Sonia Levitin. Illlustrated
by Charles Robinson.
Macmillan, 1986. 150
pages. (0-689-71130-1)

Levitin has done a fine job of portraying the hardship endured by even the more fortunate Jewish families able to escape Hitler's Germany before the full horror of WWII was unleashed. When in 1936 the Nazis passed a law denying Jewish children the right to attend public school, pre-teen Liza Platt, her parents, and two sisters emigrated to Brazil but were soon driven home by heat, illness, and the hope that the situation in Berlin had improved. By 1938, however, when Liza cannot make her way to and from school without witnessing brown-shirted students singing of planned atrocities, Mr. Platt makes up his mind to sail for America, leaving the others behind until he can make arrangements for them to join him. The focus of this novel is the anguish Liza suffers because of her father's absence and the trauma of leaving behind her extended family, friends, and all but a few belongings so that she, her mother, and sisters can escape to the safer environment of Switzerland where they must wait to hear from Mr. Platt. During the months spent in Switzerland, poverty and illness break up the Platt family for a time, but the kindness of several Swiss families sees them through until they can board ship for the U.S. With its soft black and white drawings and highly readable text, this novel is a good vehicle for teaching younger students about the European Jewish experience on a personal level.

Journey Home. Yoshiko
Uchida. Illustrated by
Charles Robinson.
Aladdin, 1978. 131 pages.
(0-689-70755-X)

With a vividness not to be found on the pages of a traditional social studies textbook, the consequences of the shameful treatment of Japanese Americans during WWII is powerfully driven home in this realistic account of the Sakane family's endeavor to rebuild a life shattered by their internment in Topaz concentration camp. Told primarily from the perspective of twelve-year-old Yuki, the novel impresses upon the reader both the nature of the hardships faced by the Sakanes and the strength which allows them finally to come home, both physically and emotionally. As Mr. Sakane says, "*Shikata ga nai.* It can't be helped. Some people have lost everything, and young men have lost their lives in this war. At least I'm alive and healthy and that's something to be thankful for." It is this attitude along with courage, perseverance, and the help provided by friends — both Japanese and Caucasian — that sustains them through racial attacks and financial recovery. Robinson's occasional but strategically placed black and white drawings heighten the impact made by this emotion-packed story, which has great potential for stimulating classroom activities focused on the causes and consequences of racism, Japanese-American history, and WWII. (*Journey Home* is the sequel to *Journey to Topaz*; see below.)

Journey to Topaz.
Yoshiko Uchida.
Illustrated by Donald Carrick. Creative Arts Book Co., 1985. 149 pages. (0-916870-85-5)

Uchida's well-crafted narrative exposes the hardships suffered by Japanese Americans who were "imprisoned by [their] own country during World War II, not because of anything [they] had done, but simply because [they] looked like the enemy." With the book's focus on the experiences of the Sakane family, eleven-year-old Yuki in particular, the events of this national tragedy are made specific and personal. The story opens on December 7, 1941, the Sakanes having just received news of the attack on Pearl Harbor. Within hours, their house has been invaded by policemen and FBI agents who arrest Mr. Sakane and eventually send him to an Army Internment Camp in Montana. Not long after, Mrs. Sakane, Yuki, and brother Kenichi learn that they must dispose of most of their belongs in preparation for removal from their home in Berkeley to nearby Tanoforan Assembly Center where they spend many weeks living in a converted horse stall. Matters worsen when they are again relocated, this time to the unfinished barracks of Topaz Concentration Camp, located in Utah's harsh Sevier desert. At the end of the story, Kenichi volunteers for military service in a special all-Nisei combat unit while the rest of the family prepare for their release from Topaz, never having relinquished their dignity or compassion for others.

Keepers of the Earth: Native American Stories and Environmental Activities for Children.
Michael J. Caduto and Joseph Bruchac.

See page 70 for entry.

The Kingdom by the Sea.
Robert Westall. Farrar
Straus Giroux, 1992. 176
pages. (0-374-34205-9)

Pleasure for the most sophisticated of readers is to be found in the rich texture of this novel, which does justice to the often startling juxtaposition of beauty and ugliness that can characterize times of tragedy. Ample helpings of both these extremes are doled out to twelve-year-old Briton Harry Baguely who, believing his family has perished during a WWII air raid, decides to strike out on his own. Roaming the Northumbrian coast with the trusty stray dog he befriends, Harry endures run-ins with the churning sea, suspicious townspeople, a shot-gun wielding farmer, and a pedophile, not to mention hunger, cold, and rain. But he also delights in the glory of sunny days, the comfort provided by his canine comrade, and his associations with an odd assortment of kind-hearted adults who offer companionship and the ever-so-welcome satisfying meal. Eventually Harry is reunited with his family members who he discovers, at least in body, have survived the German bombing. This reunion, however, proves to be a mixed blessing. After having enjoyed a sense of freedom and new maturity afforded him by the months he spent as a "pilgrim" journeying in his "kingdom by the sea," Harry wonders if he can tolerate life with people who not only have been ravaged by the war but who don't understand the transformations he has undergone. This excellent ALA Best Book for Young Adults will give students a better understanding of both the British war experience and human nature in general.

The Lady of Guadalupe.
Tomie dePaola. Holiday
House, 1980. 45 pages.
(0-8234-0403-X)

Our Lady of Guadalupe, the patron saint of Mexico, is said to have appeared to an Aztec farmer in the year 1531. With his distinctive art work and straight forward prose, Tomie dePaola dramatizes this event, which, according to tradition, resulted in the creation of a miraculous painting of the Virgin Mary. The story begins when the Aztec, known to Europeans as Juan Diego, is converted to Christianity. Becoming a devout Catholic, Juan worships regularly. One day when he is on his way to mass, he hears a wonderful sound coming from the hill of Tepeyac. At the top of the hill he sees a multicolored cloud out which floats the voice of a woman speaking his native language. Juan runs to the top of the hill and there encounters the vision of a lady as bright as the sun. Saying she is the Mother of God, the lady instructs Juan to tell the Bishop of Mexico he must immediately build a church on the spot where she is standing. Juan does what she has asked of him but finds the bishop requires some sign that will prove he has actually communicated with the Virgin. Eventually Juan convinces the bishop to build the church by showing him a *tilma* or cloak filled with roses of Castile, which only a miracle could have produced in the middle of winter. Amazed by the roses, the bishop is even more impressed by the fact that the tilma has suddenly changed into a brilliant painting of the Lady of Guadalupe. This now famous painting has been viewed by millions over the years.

Land of Hope. Joan Lowery Nixon. Bantam, 1992. 172 pages. (0-553-08110-1)

"Three of my four grandparents were immigrants to this country, so writing the Ellis Island books has been especially meaningful to me," explains the author in the afterward to this affecting addition to a series that recreates both the hardship and the intense optimism that have accompanied millions in their search for the American dream. The novel begins in 1902 when the Levinsky family flees the Jewish persecution of czarist Russia. Focused on fifteen-year-old Rebekah, the action continues with the gruelling experience of crossing the ocean in the steerage of a ship packed with European emigres. Illness, filth, and fright abound but Rebeka nevertheless is able to form warm friendships with two girls — one Swedish and the other Irish, enjoy a budding romance with a mysterious flute player, and once she hears of the educational opportunities open to girls in the U.S., entertain the possibility of attending college and becoming a teacher. Unfortunately, when the Levinskys finally complete their voyage, more troubles await them. Not only must they endure the indignity of repeated examinations by Ellis Island officials but they discover that Rebeka's grandfather, who does not pass inspection, will be forced to return to Europe. Then they are faced with the prospect of working seven days a week in a shabby New York City flat that doubles as home and a sweatshop. Difficulty in adhering to Orthodox Jewish practices, intergenerational misunderstanding, and violence between ethnic gangs further complicate the picture. But through it all, hope for the future happiness persists. Teachers will find it easy and profitable to help students see the parallels between the Levinskys' experiences and the experiences of modern-day American immigrants.

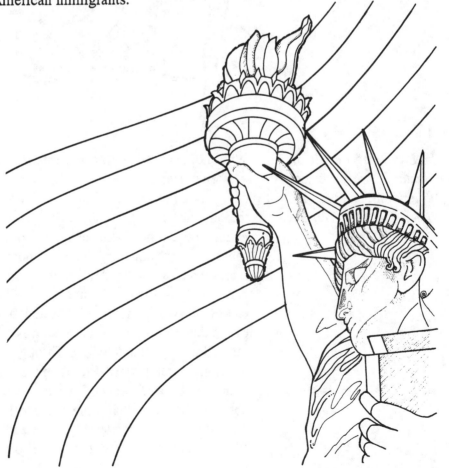

The Land I Lost: Adventures of a Boy in Vietnam. Huynh Quang Nhuong. Illustrated by Vo-Dinh Mai. J. B. Lippincott, 1982. 116 pages. (0-397-32447-2)

In this collection of biographical anecdotes, the author shares his memories of growing up in a small hamlet located on the central highlands of Vietnam. Often harshly realistic, a number of the reminiscences involve encounters with wild bore, crocodiles, or poisonous snakes which result in the injury or death of domesticated animals and humans. Others recall the process of capturing and training various animals — monkeys, songbirds, otters, and water buffalo — using a variety of techniques including addicting the animals to opiates. What seem to be the author's fondest memories revolve around his trusty water buffalo Tank and his grandmother, who not only introduced him to the opera but amazed him with her physical courage. (She repulsed bullies with karate kicks and chased off thieves with her bow and arrows.) Recipient of numerous awards — ALA Notable Children's Book, 1982; Children's Reviewer's Choice 1982; Notable Children's Trade Books in Social Studies, 1982; 1982 Teachers' Choices (NCTE); Children's Books of 1982 (Library of Congress); 1985 William Allen White Children's Book Award — Nhuong's work will make a lasting impression on students regarding a geographical area and a culture that remain a mystery to many Americans. Vo-Dinh Mai's black and white watercolor illustrations will intensify that impression.

The Land and People of Pakistan. Mark Weston. HarperCollins, 1992. 242 pages. (0-06-022789-3)

Why should we all take an interest in the country of Pakistan? Author Mark Weston presents some compelling reasons: "One out of every fifty human beings is a Pakistani. With 115 million people, Pakistan has almost half the population of the United States. It is one of the ten most populous nations on earth. Pakistan is also one of the few nations in the world capable of making nuclear weapons. . . . Few countries are as representative of the developing world as Pakistan, and this makes it particularly rewarding to study. . . . Personal income in Pakistan is very close to the world median. Pakistan is also representative of a large portion of the developing world because it is a hybrid of two great civilizations, that of India and that of Islam. Through the centuries Pakistan has belonged to empires stretching east across India as far as Bangladesh, and west across Arabia as far as Morocco. Anyone who reads about Pakistan also learns about this vast area that contains more than a quarter of the world's people." After whetting the reader's appetite with this information, Weston goes on to present clearly written, well-organized chapters on Pakistan's geography, history, economy, education, daily and family life, food, and arts and entertainment. A generous sprinkling of black and white photographs and "boxes" containing interesting supplementary information add variety to each chapter. A great source for student research, this book also contains a bibliography, filmography, and discography.

The Legend of the Bluebonnet: An Old Tale of Texas. Retold and illustrated by Tomie dePaola.

See page 32 for entry.

Let's Celebrate!: Canada's Special Days. Caroline Parry. Illustrated by Paul Baker, et al. Kids Can Press, 1987. 256 pages. (0-921103-40-9)

The title of this eclectic work fails to capture the wealth of its contents. To cover the hundreds of holidays and special events enjoyed by Canada's diverse population, Parry has written pieces ranging in length from marginal tidbits of several sentences to articles of several pages which provide information on the origins of the celebrations, the characteristics of their celebrants, and the manner in which both natives and immigrants have modified customs to give them a modern-day Canadian flavor. Organized within four major divisions based on the seasons, the writings include detailed descriptions of important religious holidays as well as individual essays providing background on world religions, for instance, Sikhism, Taoism, and Jainism. The author also presents material on such varied secular observances as Turkish Children's Day, Lesbian/Gay Pride Day, Hiroshima Day, Black History Month, Romanian Spring Festival, and Frog Follies, to name but a few. Adding to the book's fun and utility are a variety of jokes and riddles, a half dozen recipes, more than a score of art activities and games, and a generous sprinkling of black and white illustrations. Possibly most appealing is the all-embracing spirit pervading this book, a spirit which is explicitly given voice in the conclusion to Parry's discussion of calendars: "Weekly, yearly, solar, lunar, lunisolar, 'solilunar,' Gregorian, Julian — in Canada we have people who use all these different calendars. That makes a calendar of Canada's special days awfully complicated — but also very full and interesting." Certainly this unique miscellany of multicultural fact will intrigue the older student and serve as a bountiful resource for teachers of all grade levels, especially in the planning of seasonally inspired thematic units that recognize minority traditions.

Little Brother. Allan Baillie. Illustrated by Elizabeth Honey. Viking, 1992. 144 pages. (0-670-84381-4)

One nightmare after another has destroyed the comfortable life eleven-year-old Vithy once enjoyed with his family in beautiful Sambor, Cambodia. The terror begins when the Khmer Rouge bursts into his home, abducting his doctor father. Not long after, his older brother Mang meets the same fate while Vithy, along with his mother and little sister, is forced to march for days until he reaches The Big Paddy, a large work camp southwest of Phnom Penh. Both mother and sister perish under the strain of hard work and little food. Fortunately for Vithy, Mang joins him at The Big Paddy and orchestrates their escape just in time to avoid bullets intended to dispose of prisoners the Khmer Rouge no longer wants to feed. But before the boys can begin their journey to the Thai-Cambodian border and the safety of a refugee camp, Mang is captured. This vivid, well-written novel focuses on the courage and ingenuity Vichy musters in order to make his way alone to the border where he trusts he will find Mang alive waiting for him. After months at the refugee camp, Vithy gives up all hope of ever finding Mang and accepts the offer of a camp doctor to go to Australia to live with her. A strange twist of fate finally results in the bothers' reunion in Sydney. Much can be learned from this realistic story about the geography, political turmoil, and people of Cambodia.

Look What We've Brought You from Mexico: Crafts, Games, Recipes, Stories, and Other Cultural Activities from Mexican-Americans. Phyllis Shalant. Illustrated by Patricia Wynne. Julian Messner, 1992. 48 pages. (0-671-75257-X)

Many Americans are dismayingly ignorant regarding the variety of ways Mexican culture has enriched life in the U.S. In her introduction, the author zeros in on just this point: "Bite into a chocolate bar and what country do you think of? Switzerland? Belgium? France? Like most people, you'll probably be surprised to learn that chocolate is actually a gift to the world from the Indians of ancient Mexico. Today, we take for granted many other contributions from Mexican history and culture as well." Given a chance to enjoy this book with its numerous black and white drawings, students will be less likely to dismiss these contributions as well as pick up interesting facts about Mexican-American culture. To begin with, some basic information is presented regarding Mexican geography and history. Then several holidays celebrated in the U.S. by Mexican Americans are described. These include the Christmas pageants known as posadas, El Día de los Muertos (Day of the Dead), and Mexican Independence Day. In each case, readers are encouraged to enjoy some of the traditions attached to these celebrations, for example, by following the directions for making a star piñata and then playing a piñata game accompanied by the singing of Canción de la Piñata for which music and words have been provided. Reader participation is also encouraged by the presentation of several traditional recipes and the directions for games such as the sea serpent, Doña Blanca, and Indian Kickball. Finally, readers are invited to try writing with Aztec hieroglyphs and perform some arithmetic with Mayan numbers.

Lupita Mañana. Patricia Beatty. Beech Tree Books, 1992. 190 pages. (0-688-11497-0)

Possibly for the first time, students reading this realistic novel will be able to attach names and individual personalities to the human beings variously referred to as "undocumented workers," "illegal aliens," "wet backs," or worse. They will meet thirteen-year-old Lupita and her fifteen-year-old brother Salvador whose newly widowed mother has insisted they leave their Mexican village and head for the U.S. in search of jobs. Brother and sister manage to survive an attack by Mexican robbers and the gunfire of *gringo* bandits, as well as hunger, thirst, and miles of trudging through the desert. And what is their reward? They do succeed in reaching their destination, the town of Indio, California, where they had expected to be welcomed into the home of a wealthy aunt. But once in Indio, they discover a situation much different than they had anticipated. The aunt, who is crammed into a small house with six children and an unemployed husband, demands that Lupita and Salvador supplement her welfare check by paying rent. Soon Lupita and Salvador are laboring in the fields for two dollars an hour so as earn the rent and a few dollars for sending home to their mother. Besides the hard work and low pay, they must endure the constant threat of raids conducted by U.S. immigration authorities. Filled with specific detail, this novel humanizes a segment of American society that is difficult to ignore, given its ever-increasing size. An afterword written by Lucas Guttentag, Director of the Immigrants' Rights Project for the ACLU, will challenge students to examine their attitudes regarding "illegal aliens."

Malcolm X: By Any Means Necessary. Walter Dean Myers. Scholastic, 1993. 211 pages. (0-590-46484-1)

Award-winning author Walter Dean Myers offers a colorful portrait of the multidimensional Malcolm X — beloved child and promising student, drop out and petty criminal, controversial spokesman for the Nation of Islam, internationally recognized leader of African Americans. Notable for its attempt to untangle for young adult readers the complex interaction between personal and social circumstance which produced the enigmatic Malcolm, this book fruitfully mingles anecdote with history instruction. In his concluding chapter, Myers explains the dilemma he faced in undertaking an analysis of Malcolm and its ultimate resolution: "Malcolm's life seems so varied, [sic] he did so many things over the far too short thirty-nine years of his life, that it almost appears that there was not one Malcolm at all, but four distinct people. But in looking at Malcolm's life, in examining the expectations against what he actually did, we see a blending of the four Malcolms into one dynamic personality that is distinctively American in its character. For only a black man living in America could have gone through what Malcolm went through." With its well-paced narrative, plentiful photographs, and helpful time line that places incidents in Malcolm's life within the context of larger historical events, this biography more than adequately provides insight into "what Malcolm went through."

The Most Beautiful Place in the World. Ann Cameron. Illustrated by Thomas B. Allen. Knopf, 1988. 57 pages. (0-394-89463-4)

Life for Juan has been anything but beautiful though he has spent all his seven years in the mountains of San Pablo, Guatemala, a region of spectacular landscapes. Juan's problems began when his father abandoned his teenage mother: "After I was born, my dad wanted to go out with his friends at night the way he did when he was single, and my mother said there wasn't enough money for that, so they fought, and one day my dad just left." When his mother decides to remarry, she too abandons Juan to move in with her new husband: "She was going to go live with him. But I couldn't go with her. He didn't want me. He wanted to start his own family." To earn his keep, Juan helps his grandmother run her small business selling *arroz con leche* and later works by himself shining shoes. All the while Juan wonders if anybody really cares about him — maybe, he thinks, his grandmother is willing to keep him around only for the money he earns. So unsure about his grandmother's love is Juan that he is afraid to ask her to help him fulfill his dream of going to school. Eventually, he gets up the courage to broach the subject of school with her, and before long Juan is a top student. One day when his grandmother shows her admiration for his academic accomplishments, Juan is finally convinced she loves him and realizes that "where you love somebody a whole lot, and you know that person loves you, that's the most beautiful place in the world." With its soft pencil drawings, this touching story will comfort and bolster the confidence of students who have had experiences similar to Juan's.

Musical Games for Children of All Ages. Esther L. Nelson.

See page 35 for entry.

My Name Is Paula Popowich! Monica Hughes. Illustrated by Leoung O'Young. James Lorimer & Co., 1983. 150 pages. (0-88862-689-4)

Even though she loves her pale Bavarian blond mother, Paula Herman yearns to know something of the father she believes must have been the source of her own dark hair and high cheek bones. But Mrs. Herman avoids speaking of Paula's father and, in fact, has never introduced the twelve-year-old to any of her relatives, either maternal or paternal. For as long as Paula can remember, it has been just the two of them, eking by on her mother's wages as a Toronto hairdresser. But suddenly everything changes when Mrs. Herman inherits her mother's home in Alberta. She and Paula are soon on a bus headed for Edmonton where the clues Paula needs to piece together her past lie waiting for her in the attic of her new home. An old photograph reveals that her looks did in deed come from her Ukrainian Canadian father, a fact that gives Paula a comforting sense of connectedness. Unfortunately, Paula also learns that the handsome man in the picture deserted his wife and infant daughter and six years later was killed in an accident. But along with this bitter truth comes the sweetness of meeting a maternal grandmother who unites Paula with her Ukrainian heritage: "My father was dead after all, but then he had never really belonged to me except in my imagination. But now I had a real live Grandmother and instead of being a stranger I was suddenly part of Edmonton and part of what it was to be Ukrainian. I was part of Pysanki and poppyseed cookies, part of the dance." Acclaimed Canadian author Monica Hughes has written a novel that will encourage students to take an interest in their own cultural roots.

My Place. Nadia Wheatley and Donna Rawlins. Kane/Miller Book Publishers, 1992. 45 pages. (0-916291-42-1)

History takes on a human face in this unusual and fascinating work of fact-based fiction. Beginning in 1988 and regressing in ten-year increments, students are taken slowly back in time to the eighteenth century when Aborigines were still the only inhabitants of an area that today lies south of the heart of Sydney, Australia. At each stop along this reverse journey, a different youngster describes the area and his life there. On a childish map, he also has recorded what he considers to be the most interesting features of his environment. These points-of-interest are labelled with comments such as "My friend Sonia lives here," "More old brick pits. Mareka and I have adventures in them," "The soft drink factory is shut down," "Sam sometimes rides off this way to get kangaroo. He and the convicts eat it but mother and us don't." The cumulative effect, something akin to riding in a time machine, will generate in students a genuine interest in watching changes in the human and physical environment as they take place over the years. Though this well-illustrated book would be wonderful for teaching students about the development of the region around Sydney, more importantly it has the potential to spark interest in the study of history in general.

The Native American Book of Change. White Deer of Autumn. Illustrated by Shonto Begay. Beyond Words Publishing, 1992. 88 pages. (0-941831-73-6)

White Deer of Autumn, a.k.a., Gabriel Horn, a Native American teacher, activist, and author has produced an eclectic work divided into two distinct parts. Part I mingles history with prophesy. Horn explains that various Native Americans predicted the disastrous European invasion long before it occurred. Quoting many poets and prophets, Horn gives examples of the relationship between their predictions and the historical events that took place after the arrival of the conquistadors. He also cites examples of prophecies made in our own times, for instance, the Iroquoian prophecy of Deganawida. Horn's conclusion regarding modern-day prophesies? "Whether or not we choose to believe them, one thing is certain: They do shake us up. Maybe that is what we need. These are warnings. Humans must learn from the past. We must learn to live more respectfully, in balance with this earth and sky and with each other, and we must do it soon." In Part II of the book, Horn takes his reader into a sixth grade classroom where, over a period of days, he leads his students through an effective series of exercises designed to show them firsthand how it feels to have racial slurs puncture their self-esteem. In the end, he reveals to his students that he is Native American. Speaking of himself in the third person, he writes: "Mr. Horn held out his hand. 'I want you to look at the color of my hand.' Everybody did. 'This is the hand of a Native American. It is not red, or even tan. Although I have other racial blood mixed in my veins too, I am a Native American because of my heart.'" Much that is interesting and full of wisdom can be found in this unusual work.

Native American Doctor: The Story of Susan LaFlesche Picotte. Jeri Ferris. Carolrhoda Books, 1991. 88 pages. (0-87614-548-9)

More than the story of just one courageous woman's life, this biography vivifies the challenges faced by most Native Americans during the late 19th and early 20th centuries. Born in 1865 on a Nebraska reservation, Susan LaFlesche, even as a young girl, was keenly aware of the hardships suffered by her people, the once proud Omahas whose way of life had been decimated with the slaughter of the buffalo and the appropriation of their lands. She noticed in particular the lack of skill displayed by the reservation doctor and, even worse, his seeming indifference regarding the welfare of her people. Convinced that she must succeed in the white world in order to improve life for the Omahas, Susan devoted herself to acquiring an education, eventually earning a medical degree. From age 24 until her death at 50, she worked tirelessly as doctor, nurse, translator, personal advisor, cook, advocate, crusader against alcohol, missionary, wife and mother, frequently driving herself to the point of illness. Written in a clean, direct style and enriched with photographs, maps, explanatory notes, and an index, this book is a must for the study of Native American history.

Next-Door Neighbors. Sarah Ellis. Dell, 1992. 154 pages. (0-440-40620-X)

Twelve-year-old Canadian Peggy Davies moves to a new town with just four weeks left until summer vacation begins. Peggy does not relish the prospect of having to make new friends so close to the end of the school year, but before she has time to feel much discomfort, two special people enter her life. First, there is George Slobodkin, who emigrated from Russia only two and a half years ago. Though all the children, including Peggy, consider George rather odd, Peggy comes to realize that the most unusual thing about him is his extreme honesty. This Peggy likes, so she decides to invite George over despite his "weird" speech and dress, both of which have made him an easy target for the neighborhood bullies. Soon Peggy and George have decided to spend the summer preparing for a puppet show contest. Enter friend number two — Sing Lee. The gardener and cook for Peggy's new neighbor Mrs. Manning, Sing begins helping Peggy and George with their puppetry. Unfortunately, Mrs. Manning considers Sing's friendship with Peggy improper — after all, she reasons, Sing is Chinese and a grown man and thus must have ulterior motives in befriending a young white girl. In the end, Peggy and George win the contest, but Sing is fired for having attended their performance. Peggy tries to talk Mrs. Manning into reconsidering the firing but learns that the stubborn woman can't see beyond her racist view that Sing is just an inexcusably disobedient Chinese houseboy. Set in the late 1950s, this School Library Journal Best Book for Children exudes lively humor even as it teaches the sober lesson that ethnic origins need form no barrier to true friendship.

Night on Neighborhood Street. Eloise Greenfield.

See page 36 for entry.

Now Is Your Time! The African-American Struggle for Freedom. Walter Dean Myers. HarperCollins, 1991. 292 pages. (0-06-024370-8)

Here is a tour through American history as viewed from an African American perspective. Having been exposed to this perspective, students of all races will develop a richer understanding of what it means to be a American; as Meyers explains, though "events of the past cannot change, they can change in our perception of them, and in our understanding of what they mean to us today." This Coretta Scott King Award winning book opens with chapters that explore the connection between the situations in Europe, Africa, and the New World and the evolution of slavery. Later chapters examine the roles African Americans have played in the development of the United States from Revolutionary times up through the civil rights movement of the 1960s. Along the way, Myers has done an admirable job of interweaving information about individuals into the broad cloth of history. For example, in attempting to enlighten readers as to the effect slavery could have on individual human beings, Myers devotes an entire chapter to the life of Abd al-Rahman Ibrahima, a well-educated Fula prince who spent twenty years in bondage working for a farmer in the Mississippi Territory before Secretary of State Henry Clay secured his release. Myers also integrates facts he uncovered during his research that pertain to the lives of his own ancestors. The end result is a work that turns history into a engrossing story, which Myers has augmented with photographs, historical documents, and a bibliography. Comparisons between traditional American history texts and this book could lead to discussions and writing projects that would develop students' critical thinking skills as well as help them realize that history is open to various interpretations.

One Day in the Tropical Rainforest. Jean Craighead George. Illustrated by Gary Allen. Thomas Y. Crowell, 1990. (0-690-04767-3)

Tepui, a Native South American boy, must race against the clock to save his way of life. In order to stop the bulldozers that have come to destroy his home — the lush Venezuelan rainforest — he must find a rare butterfly. Only then will a wealthy benefactor agree to purchase the forest and set it aside as the International Tropical Rain Forest of the Macaw. Newberry Medalist Jean Craighead George has written a fictional but highly realistic minute-by-minute account of Tepui's quest for the butterfly:

"8:15 A.M. . . . . Tepui stepped off the porch. Taking a bearing on the tallest tree in the rain forest, he led Dr. Rivero off along the Trail of the Potoo.

"9:00 A.M. The bulldozer drivers, truck drivers, and chain sawyers got back in their vehicles and rolled again.

"9:30 A.M.   The butterfly shook fluid into her wings, and they opened like flower petals. Iridescent purple 'eyes' appeared in a metallic-blue field on her forewings. . . ."

Allen's detailed pencil drawings will help students visualize the rich plant and animal life that Tepui wants so badly to preserve and that the author describes so accurately in this story.

One More River to Cross: The Stories of Twelve Black Americans. Jim Haskins. Scholastic, 1992. 215 pages. (0-590-42896-9)

In his introduction Haskins declares that "from music to science to law to business to politics, there are few if any areas of American and world life that have not been touched and made better by black Americans." The twelve biographical essays that follow provide just the kind of evidence needed to demonstrate the truth of this assertion. Achievement in the face of racism, sexism, and/or poverty provides the unifying theme for this inspirational work that illuminates the lives of Crispus Attucks, hero of the Boston Massacre; Madam C. J. Walker, millionaire entrepreneur; Matthew Henson, co-discoverer of the North Pole; Marian Anderson, opera star; Ralph Bunche, winner of the Nobel Peace Prize; Dr. Charles R. Drew, innovator in the field of hematology; Romare Bearden, outstanding twentieth century artist; Fannie Lou Hamer, civil rights leader; Eddie Robinson, legendary football coach; Shirley Chisholm, former member of Congress and political activist; Malcolm X, civil rights leader; and Dr. Ronald McNair, space shuttle astronaut. A black and white portrait accompanying each essay and Haskins' ability to put the lives of these heros into a historical context without weighing down his prose with unnecessarily long-winded explanations will attract students hungry for information that should be common knowledge to all Americans.

The Pacific Islanders.
Douglas Ford. Chelsea
House, 1989. 111 pages.
(0-87754-883-8)

As senior consulting editor to the extensive series *The Peoples of North America* of which this book is a part, Senator Daniel Patrick Moynihan has written a fine introductory essay outlining the history of immigration to both the U.S. and Canada and stating the guiding principle behind the series: "The people of North America are the descendants of one of the greatest migrations in history. And that migration is not over. . . . To understand ourselves, we must know something about our diverse ethnic ancestry. Nothing so defines the North American nations as the motto on the Great Seal of the United States: *E Pluribus Unum* — Out of Many, One." This particular book begins with a chapter that explains the unique status held by many Pacific Island immigrants. Unlike other groups, "Pacific Islanders found themselves in possession of many — if not all — of the rights and privileges of American citizens before setting foot outside their homeland." This situation arose out of the fact that the United States has had close political ties with many Pacific Island countries such as the Hawaiian Islands, Guam, and Samoa. The second chapter defines the Pacific Island region as that approximately one third of the Pacific Ocean containing Polynesia, Micronesia, and Melanesia. Succeeding chapters explore the history and cultures of some of the varied peoples found on these islands. A final chapter discusses what life is like in the U.S. today for Pacific Islanders, many of whom have had to struggle with acculturation and the American tendency to lump them together with Asians as one homogeneous group. Numerous photographs round out this instructive work.

The People Could Fly:
American Black Folktales.
Retold by Virginia
Hamilton.

See page 38 for entry.

A Proud Taste for Scarlet
and Miniver. E. L.
Koningsburg. Macmillan,
1973. 201 pages.
(0-689-30111-1)

The life and times of Eleanor of Aquitaine provide the basic subject matter for this highly entertaining historical fantasy. From it much can be learned about the ambitious Eleanor's deeds as the influential queen of both Louis VII of France and Henry II of England, but a dry chronicle of twelfth century Western European history this is not. Koningsburg has taken biographical fact and applied to it imagination and humor. Eleanor's story unfolds in a series of four tales, one of which is told by the deceased queen herself and the other three by people who knew her intimately during her lifetime. For Eleanor and her friends, all residents of Heaven, the tales serve as a means of amusing themselves as they await the ascension of Henry II, who has been compelled to serve more than six centuries in Hell redeeming himself before he can join them. But it is not this fantastic scenario which gives charm to this work as much as it is the colorful characterizations and amusing dialogue that make flesh and blood a variety of important figures from the past. A case in point — in speaking of her newly crowned son Richard the Lion Heart, the outspoken Eleanor declares, "The English will claim him for theirs, and they will love him, even if he can't speak their language. He ought to learn it though. . . . English is a strong language. It has a great assortment of four-letter words." Having enjoyed Koningsburg's lively text and detailed illustrations, students will surely find themselves wanting to investigate further not only Eleanor herself but Arthurian legend, the traditions of courtly love, the geography and aristocracy of medieval Europe, the Crusades, jousting tournaments, and a whole host other European cultural features mentioned in this Junior Library Guide selection that was chosen as an outstanding book for older readers.

The Road to Memphis. Mildred D. Taylor. Dial Books, 1990. 290 pages. (0-8037-0340-6)

This sequel to *Roll of Thunder, Hear My Cry* finds Cassie Logan, now seventeen, involved in predicaments that she and her older brother Stacey endeavor to handle without parental intervention. Cassie, like any young person, is attempting to come to terms with classic adolescent concerns: her family's expectations that she begin to play the part of the feminine young lady, the attentions of a marriage-minded young man, her desire to help patch up the life of an unwed pregnant friend, and her dream of completing her education all the way through college and law school. But unlike many youths, she must also contend with a whole host of problems that are the direct outgrowth of racial injustice: threatened arrest for her attempt to use a rest room designated for "White Ladies Only," the injury of a friend forced to play the part of the "coon" in a sadistic hunting expedition, and the possibility that another friend will be convicted for assaulting three whites who tormented him until he could not keep from retaliating. Again Taylor has delivered a gripping narrative that speaks volumes about the ugliness of Southern racism and its catastrophic consequences for both blacks and whites.

Roll of Thunder, Hear My Cry. Mildred D. Taylor. Bantam, 1989. 210 pages. (0-553-25450-2)

Distinctive characterizations and a fast-paced plot will certainly hold students' interest as they delve into the lives of the Logan clan, a cohesive African American family grappling with the pervasive racism of rural Mississippi during the 1930s. The narrator, Cassie Logan, relates the events of the novel in the voice of a thoughtful adult though she is only nine-years-old at the time the story opens and just beginning to comprehend the reality of living in an unjust world. In the course of only one year, she becomes fully awakened to the existence of a variety of oppressors: a bus driver who takes pleasure in splattering young black students with red mud as he speeds toward the all-white school; a white girl who feels she is entitled to order Cassie off the sidewalk and into the gutter; "night riders" who roam the countryside killing and maiming; and a white power structure that is bent upon cheating African Americans out of all it can, including the precious four hundred acres that have been owned by the Logan family since the time of Reconstruction. But most important, during this year Cassie also discovers the determination and bravery with which her family and friends can work together in the fight against such oppression. Reading Taylor's Newbery Medal winner will enable students to grasp the horror of post-Civil War racial persecution as well as develop an appreciation for the "ordinary" African Americans who have acted with courage and dignity in the struggle for justice.

Rose Blanche. Roberto Innocenti and Christophe Gallaz. Stewart, Tabori & Chang, 1990. 26 pages. (1-55670-207-8)

Textbook chapters on the Holocaust may give students an intellectual grasp of the horrendous events that took place. But this fictional work, without resorting to graphic detail, will let them *feel* the events. They will listen with horror as a young German girl describes from the point of view of an uncomprehending innocent the progressive control the Nazis exert over the lives around her. Rose Blanche begins her story with a chilling misinterpretation of what really is taking place: "One day the first truck arrived and many men left. They were dressed like soldiers. Winter was beginning. Now the trucks follow each other under the school windows. They are full of soldiers we don't know, but they wink at us.... The trucks are fun to watch. We stand in the doorway as they pass. We don't know where they're going. But we think they're going someplace on the other side of the river." It is not long before Rose Blanche finds out the truth. One cold day she sees a boy grabbed by a soldier and stuffed into one of the trucks. She decides to follow it into the forest where she comes upon an electrified barbed wire fence. Behind the fence are starving children. Rose Blanche begins making secret trips into the forest to bring them food, keeping it up until the day soldiers mistake her for one of the enemy: "Rose Blanche's mother waited a long time for her little girl. The crocuses finally sprang up from the ground. The river swelled and overflowed its banks. Trees were green and full of birds." But Rose Blanche was never to return. A stark, powerful text and exquisite art work are combined in this American Library Association Notable Children's Book and Horn Book Honor List designee.

Sadako and the Thousand Paper Cranes. Eleanor Coerr. Illustrated by Ronald Himler. Putnam's, 1977. 64 pages. (0-399-20520-9)

Since 1958 a statue of a young Japanese girl named Sadako Sasaki has stood in Hiroshima Peace Park. This beautifully written book tells Sadako's story. Author Eleanor Coerr gathered her information from actual letters Sadako wrote to her classmates as she lay dying of cancer caused by atomic radiation. Coerr has shaped this material into a sensitive narrative that opens on August 6, 1954. At this point Sadako is still a vigorous eleven-year-old with mixed emotions about attending another of the ceremonies conducted in memory of those who perished in the bombing. At the Peace Park, Sadako recoils at the sight of photographs taken after the explosion and recalls her own impression of the event: "'I remember the Thunderbolt,' Sadako whispered to her friend. 'There was the flash of a million suns. Then the heat prickled my eyes like needles.'" Little does Sadako know that before long she herself will become another victim of Hiroshima. After a few months when dizzy spells have become increasingly frequent, Sadako visits a hospital and is diagnosed with leukemia. During Sadako's decline, she remains optimistic and continues for as long as she is able to make the origami birds her friend Chizuko has told her will save her: "'Don't you remember that old story about the crane?' Chizuko asked. 'It's supposed to live for a thousand years. If a sick person folds one thousand paper cranes, the gods will grant her wish and make her healthy again.'" Before her death, Sadako completed 644 cranes. This intensely moving story is illustrated with graceful black and white paintings.

Secret of the Andes. Ann Nolan Clark. Puffin Books, 1976. 120 pages. (0-14-030926-8)

Set in and around beautiful Hidden Valley, a remote spot in the Peruvian Andes, this well-crafted novel follows the adventures of eight-year-old Cusi, a descent of the Incas. For as long as he can remember, Cusi has lived in the company of his beloved llamas and only one other human being, a wise old man named Chuto. Content with his life until recently, Cusi has begun to wonder about his origins and the outside world. All that he understands of human relationships, besides his bond with Chuto, comes from having observed one Native American family camped far below his mountain home. But even this glimpse has opened up a yearning, which is only intensified when Chuto takes Cusi on his first journey beyond confines of Hidden Valley. As they rest beside some Incan ruins, Cusi is flooded with questions and emotion: "Was he of ancient [Incan] nobility? ... Did the royal blood of ancient kings still flow in the veins of his people? Again Cusi felt a vague unknown trouble like a cloud over the sun of a happy day. Again he felt a longing in his heart. Was it for kinship? Was it for family? How could he miss what he had not known?" By the end of the story, Cusi has come to a difficult decision: he will give up the idea of looking to the outside world for his future happiness and remain with Chuto in Hidden Valley to carry on the traditions of his Incan forebears. In reading Clark's sensitive, well-researched Newbery Award winner, students will learn something of the Incan culture and the struggle to preserve it.

Shabanu: Daughter of the Wind. Suzanne Fisher Staples. Knopf, 1989. 240 pages. (0-394-84815-2)

According to Islamic tradition, girls of Pakistan's Cholistan desert are destined for arranged marriages and motherhood well before the age of sixteen. Such is the case for the protagonist, twelve-year-old Shabanu, who loves the open spaces of the desert and caring for the camels that are so much a part of her life. For Shabanu, the inevitability of her own marriage colors all she sees and does. Observing the mating behavior of an young male camel brings to mind the image of a future husband who will expect submissive obedience. And as she watches her older sister Phulan struggle to adjust to reality of her up-coming wedding, Shabanu can't help but think of her own fate: "There has been no more crying under the quilt. As Muslim girls, we are brought up knowing our childhood homes are temporary. Our real homes are the ones we go to when we marry. I wonder how I can ever accept a place outside the desert, without my camels and Mama and Dadi." After Phulan's wedding, Shabanu works up the courage to run off in a desperate attempt to avoid marriage to a man she feels sure will bring her sadness. But when one of her camels breaks its leg, she faces the fact that her escape is impossible and stoically takes a beating from her father. She derives strength from the thought that her future husband will never be able to take away her innermost beauty: he "will reach out to me for the rest of his life and never unlock the secrets of my heart." A novel for mature readers, this revealing work has been named a NewBery Honor Book, an ALA Best Book for Young Adults, and a *New York Times* Notable Book of the Year.

The Shadow Brothers. A. E. Cannon. Delacorte Press, 1990. 181 pages. (0-385-29982-6)

Sixteen-year-old Marcus Jenkins proves to be a sensitive yet wry, thoroughly likable first person-narrator for this well-written novel focused on the friendship between the Anglo Marcus and his Navajo foster brother Henry. As far as Marcus has been concerned, he and the gifted Henry could not have been closer, having shared the same room, family, and activities for almost a decade. He certainly has never let himself entertain two disturbing possibilities: one, that he could feel envious of Henry's achievements; or two, that Henry has ever felt anything but comfortable and happy since he left an Arizona reservation to come and live with the Jenkins family in suburban Utah. But as the novel progresses, Marcus learns that he has been blind to both of these realities. He finally admits to himself that fear of competing with Henry accounts for his lackadaisical approach to his school work and track practice. And even more devastating, Marcus discovers that Henry, though he loves the Jenkins, has suffered all these years from a deep loneliness, which he never cared to share with Marcus, a loneliness driven by a longing for the father, grandfather, and Navajo culture he left behind. This Junior Library Guild outstanding book for young adults humanizes the pain that may be encountered, even under the best of circumstances, when members of a minority culture are expected to become part of the dominant culture at the expense of their heritage. Living in a multicultural society is just one of the many themes teachers can explore with their students as they read this multidimensional book.

Shake It to the One That You Love the Best: Play Songs and Lullabies from Black Musical Traditions. Collected and adapted by Cheryl Warren Mattox.

For entry see page 40.

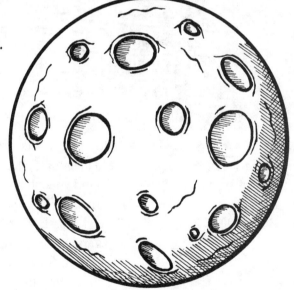

Sing Down the Moon. Scott O'Dell. Dell, 1976. (0-440-97975-7)

"The sky was gray and the air smelled of bitter winds. The Long Knives drove us along the river and through the portals of the canyon. Like sheep before the shepherd, we went without a sound."

Observations of the young Native American narrator of O'Dell's stirring novel, these words describe the forced relocation of thousands of Navahos carried out by "Long Knives," i.e., American soldiers. Compelled to leave behind the natural beauty of northeastern Arizona's canyon country where sheep herding had sustained them, the narrator and her family are driven far south into the dry lands of southern New Mexico. Following their anguishing journey, they spend month after month under the watchful eyes of the Long Knives. Then one day the girl and her new husband make a daring escape back to their former homelands, just in time for the birth of their baby. Powerfully described from the Native American perspective, these events are based upon historical facts O'Dell discusses in his "Postscript": "In June 1863 the United States sent Colonel Kit Carson through the Navaho country. . . with instructions to destroy all crops and livestock. . . . Word was sent out that all Navahos were to give themselves up, and early in 1864 they began to surrender. By March they had started on their long journey to Fort Sumner, 180 miles southeast of Santa Fe . . . This 300-mile journey of the Navahos is known as The Long Walk. To this day, Navaho men and women speak of it with bitterness." O'Dell's Newberry Honor Book will pass on to students a part of American history that has much to teach.

The Snow Queen. Hans Christian Andersen.

See page 41 for entry.

A Thief in the Village and Other Stories. James Berry. Puffin Books, 1990. 148 pages. (0-14-034357-1)

Readers of this colorful short story collection will find themselves amidst the lush natural beauty of the Caribbean, listening to the distinctive rhythms of island speech and sharing in the dreams and pain of a variety of young Jamaicans. They will meet Becky, who wants more than anything else to own a bike. But first she must overcome obstacles in the shape of poverty and gender stereotypes: "Becky, I heard you mother tell you over and over she can't afford to buy you a bike. Yet you keep on and on. Child, you're a girl." Then there is Fanso, a boy longing to hear something about the father he has never known. When he persists in asking his grandmother about the man, she lets him have the truth: "Fanso, mi Son-Son--much I could tell you. But--all I'll say is, you father born bad. Bad, bad! He never was anyt'ing good." Perhaps most memorable of Berry's protagonists is Gustus. So intense is his desire that he is willing to brave a hurricane to tend a banana tree; only by protecting and selling its fruit does he have a chance at happiness. When his father finds Gustus lying injured at the base of the tree, he can't believe his eyes: "Mi bwoy! Mi hurricane bwoy! The Good Lord save you. . . . . Why you do this? Why you do this?" Gustus's answer touches his father deeply as it will every sensitive reader: "I did want buy mi shoes, Pappy. I. . . . I can't go anywhere 'cause I have no shoes. . . . I didn' go to school outing at the factory. I didn' go to Government House. . . ." Of the nine stories comprising this ALA Notable Book, more than one ends on a bittersweet note but each is filled with characters worth meeting.

Thirteen Moons on Turtle's Back: A Native American Year of Moons. Joseph Bruchac and Jonathan London.

See page 43 for entry.

This Same Sky: A Collection of Poems from around the World. Selected by Naomi Shihab Nye. Four Winds Press, 1992. 212 pages. (0-02-768440-7)

Editor Naomi Shihab Nye assembled this collection of 150 plus poems written by authors from sixty-eight countries without including a single one composed by an American. In the introduction, she explains her reasons for having done so: "Those of us living in the United States often suffer from a particular literary provinciality, imagining ourselves to be the primary readers and writers of the planet. We forget that our literary history is relatively brief. . . . When a writer in Dhaka, Bangladesh, said, 'We try so hard to know what people are writing in the United States--do people in your country try as hard to know about us?' I felt ashamed. . . . Because of the number of fine anthologies featuring poets from the United States that have appeared in recent years, I have decided not to include writers who were born in the United States." Teachers can help American students shed their ethnocentric blinders by sharing with them the wonderfully varied poems included in this anthology. Divided into six thematic sections--"Words and Silences," "Dreams and Dreamers," "Families," "This Earth and Sky in Which We Live," "Losses," and "Human Mysteries"--this work has something in it that will fire the imagination of almost any advanced intermediate or upper grade student. Brief biographical notes on the contributing poets and a map of the world on which their homelands have been indicated will further broaden students' horizons.

Thunderwith. Libby Hathorn. Little, Brown, and Co., 1991. (0-316-35034-6)

The death of her mother leaves fifteen-year-old Australian Laura Ritchie with two disquieting alternatives; she can take up residence in an orphanage or go to live on a farm with a father she has not seen for over a decade. Urged by her dying mother to try the latter, Laura finds herself on a piece of undeveloped land, sharing a corrugated metal shed-like structure with her dad, a stepmother, three half sisters, and an infant half brother. The relative poverty, hard work, and severe natural environment that characterize her new life in the Wallingat rain forest of New South Wales do not disturb Laura much. However, she is devastated by the cold hostility with which her stepmother Gladwym treats her even though the gentle girl has shown herself to be a diligent worker and a loving half sister. So extreme is Gladwyn's rejection that she expresses no appreciation even after Laura succeeds in getting her to a hospital before she bleeds to death from an axe wound. Because Laura's father is gone much of the time, her only readily available source of human comfort comes from a friendship she develops with an old Aboriginal man who tells traditional Koori stories at the high school library. But Laura also finds solace in the form of a beautiful part-dingo dog that she meets on her walks in the forest. Having first encountered the animal during a violent storm, Laura calls him Thunderwith and relies on their mutual love to help ease the pain of her mother's death and her stepmother's indifference. Named an ALA Best Book for Young adults, this sensitive novel explores emotions that will seem familiar to students who have experienced the death of a parent or the challenge of establishing a relationship with a stepparent. Animal lovers and students curious about Australia's natural landscape and native culture will also enjoy this book.

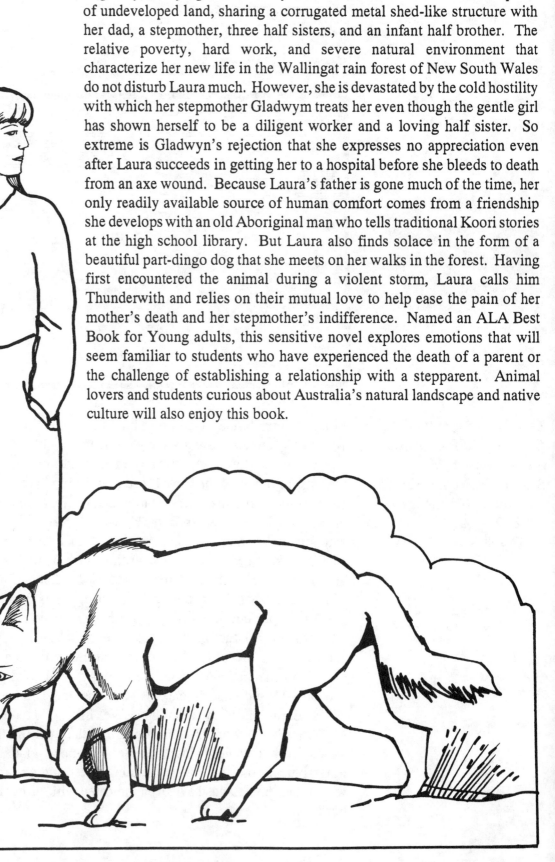

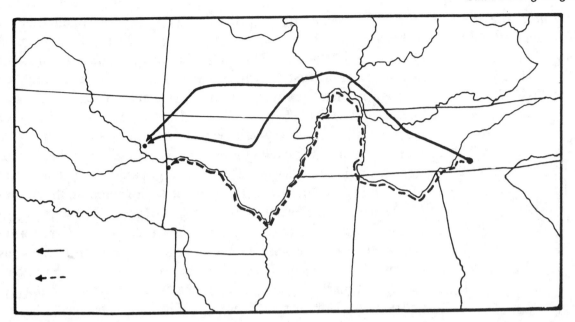

The Trail on Which They Wept: The Story of a Cherokee Girl. Dorothy and Thomas Hoobler and Carey-Greenberg Associates. Illustrated by S. S. Burrus. Silver Burdett Press, 1992. 57 pages. (0-382-24333-1)

This affecting historical novella recreates the infamous Trail of Tears from the perspective of a Cherokee girl named Sarah Tsaluh Rogers. When Sarah and her people hear rumors that President Jackson will not enforce a Supreme Court decision allowing the Cherokees to keep their land, they are stunned. "He wanted the Cherokees to move hundreds of miles west, across the Mississippi River. He said they would be happier there. Of course everyone knew that wasn't true. The Cherokees were happy right here in the land where they had always lived. It's our land! Sarah thought angrily. We won't leave it!" But leave it they must when soldiers begin evicting people from their homes. Sarah's grandmother, full of hatred for the *unakas*--white people, tells Sarah she should go by her Cherokee name, Tsaluh, instead of her *unaka* name, Sarah. The grandmother also says that she herself will not survive the trip to live on the cursed new lands the *unaka* government has promised them. Thus it is that besides having to endure the extreme physical hardship that is part of the three-hundred mile march, Sarah must also resolve an internal struggle, a battle between her two selves: Sarah, educated by English-speaking Christian missionaries and Tsaluh, taught Cherokee ways by her beloved grandmother. Though one out of four, including her grandmother, does not survive the journey, Sarah recovers from a fever and begins a new life. With the help of a spiritual advisor, the famous Cherokee leader Sequoyah, whom her grandmother had prophesied would come to her aid, Sarah learns to accept the *unaka* part of her character. The pencil drawings of Native American artist S. S. Burris make Sarah's ordeal seem all the more real.

Under the Sunday Tree. Eloise Greenfield.

See page 45 for entry.

Undying Glory: The Story of the Massachusetts 54th Regiment. Clinton Cox. Scholastic, 1991. 167 pages. (0-590-44170-1)

"Writing about the 54th," explains the author, "was like finding people who had never been allowed to tell their story, and then helping them tell it." Cox, a two-time Pulitzer Prize nominee, has done a fine job of presenting the history of the first African American regiment to have been recruited with government approval, a story that certainly deserves telling. Soon after the outbreak of the Civil War, African Americans looking forward to the eradication of slavery volunteered for military service, but local and federal authorities, including President Lincoln, rejected them as unfit to fight in a "white man's war." Thanks in large part to the determined efforts of abolitionists Frederick Douglas and Governor John Andrew of Massachusetts, the Secretary of War finally gave Andrew permission to muster troops consisting of "persons of African descent, organized into special corps." To ensure the success of his endeavors, Andrew insisted on careful screening of all recruits so that, once assembled, the 54th proved superior in many ways to white regiments with their lower literacy rates and poorer health. Despite their superiority and the fact that they had been promised equal treatment, members of the 54th discovered their pay to be less, their chances for becoming officers slim, and the respect accorded them by many Union soldiers nil. This did not, however, deter the 54th from playing an important part in the capture of Charleston and the march toward racial equality.

West Coast Chinese Boy. Sing Lim. Tundra Books, 1991. 63 pages. (0-88776-270-0)

Born in 1915, Sing Lim grew up in Vancouver, British Columbia, during a time when Chinese Canadian's were often victims of racism. The childhood memories Lim has recorded in this book are full of colorful particulars that reflect his ability to take the good along with the bad and still hold onto a zest for life. In the afterword, Lim explains the attitude that clearly shows itself in his anecdotes: "As I look back on the events of my childhood, some of which happened over sixty years ago, I feel many emotions: love and gratitude, amazement and fear, anger and frustration, but most of all, the urge to laugh. Recently, someone who knows a little of the terrible treatment suffered by Chinese Canadians through the years asked me: 'How did you survive it?' 'By laughing,' I said. 'It is the sense of humor of the Chinese that helps us live through the unlivable.'" Thus, it is that readers will hear on one page of race riots that devastated Chinatown but on another, a funny story about a Chinese opera star who was caught on stage in her underwear. They will encounter Lim's sad revelation that his gentle mother died when he was only fourteen as well as his admission that he found the pretentious funerals of wealthy Chinese highly entertaining. They will learn that Lim feared fights provoked by white kids who called Chinese "yellow bellies" but that he loved his "wonderful teacher Miss Scott," who urged him to develop his artistic talents. The ability that Miss Scott detected so long ago is evident in the many drawings that fill Lim's award-winning text.

Where Angels Glide: New Stories from Latin America. Lori M. Carlson and Cynthia L. Ventura, eds. Illustrated by José Ortega. J. B. Lippincott, 1990. 114 pages. (0-397-32425-1)

Editors Carlson and Ventura express a laudable purpose in having compiled this distinctive collection of ten short stories: "Latin American literature in English translation has been enjoyed by adult readers for over two decades. We think it is time that younger readers also have the opportunity to explore its riches. Since Latin America is a group of countries with a striking variety of climates, geographies, and cultural traditions, we have made every effort to include stories that express this remarkable diversity." Happily, they have achieved their goal. Diverse in their settings--Argentina, Chile, Puerto Rico, Cuba, Panama, Mexico, El Salvador, and Peru--the stories also reflect a variety of culturally specific preoccupations. "A Clown's Story," for instance, makes painfully clear the difficulty of carrying on with ordinary life in war-plagued El Salvador. The clown-hero ruefully admits that "nighttime in San Salvador isn't a good time for circuses. But it is for other things: arrests, assassinations, kidnappings, bombings, and torture." In the mystically beautiful "Tarma," a brother and sister contemplate the seemingly infinite age and expanse of the Pacific before ascending to a village in the Peruvian Andes to take part in traditional Easter week celebrations and then find themselves traveling back down, "down to the ocean, where the waves still [crash] on the dark sands of Lima." Ortega's black and white drawings introduce each piece and intensify the mysterious quality shared by many of the stories. Teachers will find this collection a wonderful stimulus for thought-provoking class discussion, analytic writing assignments, and students' own creative writing projects as well as a flavorful accompaniment to social studies units focused on Latin America.

Where the Buffaloes Begin. Olaf Baker. Illustrated by Stephen Gammel. Puffin Books, 1985. 35 pages. (0-14-050560-1)

How must it have been to share the open plains with millions of mighty buffalo in the days before the coming of the Europeans? The powerful prose and wonderful illustrations of this Caldecott Honor Book will give students the chance to step into the moccasins of Little Wolf, a young Native American who lived long ago, and accompany him as he rides out to the lake where, according to legend, the first buffalo originated. Once at the lake, Little Wolf lies down among the prairie grasses, confident that he will achieve his goal--to see for himself the buffalo emerge from the lake's watery depths. As the stars come out above him, he continues his patient waiting, watching, and listening. All the while, words from the buffalo legend mix with the sounds of the night: "Do you hear the noise that never ceases? It is the Buffaloes fighting far below. They are fighting to get out upon the prairie. They are born below the Water but are fighting for the Air, in the great lake in the Southland where the Buffaloes begin!" Suddenly awakening from a doze, Little Wolf realizes the animals have finally arrived and jumps to his feet: "With staring eyes he drank in the great vision. And not only with his eyes but also with his ears and nose: for his ears were filled with the trampling and snorting of the herd and the flash of the water as it moved under their hooves." Before long, Little Wolf is riding on his pony in the midst of the herd, shouting and waving his arms like a wild man. Appropriately, the hazy softness of Gammell's exquisite black and white pencil drawings creates the illusion that Little Wolf and the majestic buffalo are being viewed through the distance of many, many years.

Winter Tales from Poland.
Told by Maia
Wojciechowska.
Illustrated by Laszlo
Kubinyi. Doubleday,
1973. 65 pages.
(0-385-02839-3)

As its title suggests, this collection of eight Polish tales by Newbery Medalist Maia Wojciechowska tends to explore the dark, wintry side of life. Though the majority of the stories finish on the upbeat, such is certainly not the case with three of them, including the first, "The Angel." Opening during a time in Polish history "long before people learned how to read and write, even before they learned to hurt each other," soon the narrative proceeds to a time when the ability to hurt is all too evident. Evil prevails when a beautiful girl stands by and lets her three brothers cut the wings from an angel who loves her. The girl, we are told in the last paragraph, is doomed to live forever unless someone can find the angel and intervene on the her behalf--sadly, the story ends before that someone appears. In "Bartek the Doctor," a good-for-nothing son makes good but then must die to pay for having saved his own mother's life while in "The Freak," an odd-looking baby born to an elderly couple winds up with a bullet in his forehead. In a more hopeful vein, there are "The Test" in which a King who exiles his wife for disobedience eventually forgives her; "How a Tailor Became a King" in which a gaunt tailor mends the sky and becomes a jolly, fat monarch; "The Jester Who Learned to Cry" in which a jester finally succeeds in amusing his king but only after he has learned to cry; "Seven Black Crows" in which a mother's curse upon her sons is broken; and finally, "The Time of the Ugly" in which a man escapes the noose by ridding the land of a hideous creature. Wojciechowska's prose style and Kubinyi's expressive pencil drawings work together to produce an interesting, unusual work that reflects at least one facet of Polish tradition.

Selected Bibliography of Teacher Resources

A Calendar of Religious Holidays and Ethnic Festivals: September 1992 to 1994. New York: National Conference of Christians and Jews, Inc., 1992.
A four-page pamphlet that briefly describes and lists dates for religious and ethnic celebrations of the '92-'93 and '93-'94 school years. "Teachers may find the calendar particularly helpful because it contains festivals that can be occasions for objective, non-credal instruction on particular cultures."

"Caribbean Bibliography: Selected Resources for Teachers and Students." *Social Education* April/May 1991: 237-38.
Contains several dozen works grouped under the following headings: Nonfiction for Secondary Students, Background and Guides for the Instructor, and Fiction by Caribbean Authors (novels, anthologies, and poetry). Also lists sources for books and films.

Cech, Maureen. *Globalchild: Multicultural Resources for Young Children.* Menlo Park, CA: Addison-Wesley Publishing Co., 1991.
Describes numerous classroom activities designed to develop an appreciation for multiculturalism in preschool and early primary students. Contains lots of recipes and reproducible art.

Derman-Sparks, Louise and the A.B.C. Task Force. *Anti-Bias Curriculum: Tools for Empowering Young Children.* Washington, D.C.: National Assn. for the Education of Young Children, 1991.
Offers ideas and activities for introducing young children to diversity related to race, disabilities, gender, and culture. Includes a bibliography of children's books and "ten quick ways" to evaluate literature so as to avoid sexism and racism.

Educational Leadership Dec. 1991/Jan. 1992.
All the articles in this issue focus on multicultural education and together provide an interesting range of views on the subject.

Gomez-Engler, Raquel. *Broadening the Literary Canon: A Multicultural Bibliography.* La Jolla, CA: U of California, San Diego, 1991.
Compiled for the California Literature Project, this bibliography provides very brief annotations describing over 150 works of multicultural literature for children, adolescents, and adults.

Harris, Violet J., ed. *Teaching Multicultural Literature in Grades K-8.* Norwood, MA: Christopher-Gordon Publishers, 1992.
A collection of articles covering the selection and use of multicultural literature in general as well as the specific issues pertaining to African American, Asian Pacific, Native American, Puerto Rican, Mexican American, and Caribbean children's literature.

Hayden, Carla D., ed. *Ventures into Cultures: A Resource Book of Multicultural Materials and Programs.* Chicago: American Library Assn., 1992.
With a focus on "groups found in significant numbers in the United States," this anthology suggests children's books and activities that would be appropriate for teaching students of all ages about the following cultures: African American, Arabic, Asian, Hispanic, Jewish, Native American, and Persian.

Horning, Kathleen T. "Sacred Places: American Indian Literature from Small Presses." *Book Links* Sept. 1991: 16-20.
Advocates exploring small presses, many of which are owned by various Indian Nations, as a source of Native American literature that offers a perspective not found in children's trade literature. Also reviews a number of books and concludes with a twenty-five item bibliography.

Kruse, Ginny Moore, et al. *Multicultural Literature for Children and Young Adults: A Selected Listing of Books 1980-1990 by and about People of Color.* Madison, WI: Wisconsin Department of Public Instruction, 1991.
An annotated bibliography of over 450 books that have been grouped into sixteen different categories based on either theme, genre, or reader characteristics.

Lee, Galda. "Dreamtime Downunder: Exploring Australian Books." *The Reading Teacher* Oct. 1992: 146-56.
Reviews more than fifty recently published works that depict life in Australia.

--- with Donna Diehl and Lane Ware. "One World, One Family." *The Reading Teacher* Feb. 1993: 410-19.
Reviews more than sixty recently published works of multicultural literature that can "help open many worlds to young readers."

Lindgren, Merri V., ed. *The Multicolored Mirror: Cultural Substance in Literature for Children and Young Adults.* Fort Atkinson, WI: Highsmith Press, 1991.
An anthology of articles discussing issues related to multicultural literature for young people. Article topics include self-esteem development, authenticity of works, the publishing of multicultural literature, and 101 recommended books.

Miller-Lachmann, Lyn. *Our Family, Our Friends, Our World: An Annotated Guide to Significant Multicultural Books for Children and Teenagers.* New Providence, NJ: R. R. Bowker, 1992.
Divided into eighteen chapters corresponding to geographic regions of the world, this hefty volume reviews over 1,000 books published between 1970 and 1990. Within each chapter, books are grouped according to grade level, beginning with preschool and continuing through high school.

NCSS Task Force on Ethnic Studies Curriculum Guidelines. *Curriculum Guidelines for Multicultural Education: A Position Statement of National Council for the Social Studies.* Washington, DC: National Council for the Social Studies, 1991.
A twenty-page document that discusses the rationale and guidelines for developing a multicultural curriculum. Includes a detailed checklist for evaluating multicultural programs.

Pang, Valerie Ooka, et al. "Beyond Chopsticks and Dragons: Selecting Asian-American Literature for Children." *The Reading Teacher* November 1992: 216-24.
Provides criteria for selecting children's literature that will promote "sensitive, positive, and accurate portrayals" of Asian and Pacific Islander Americans. Also reviews twenty recommended books.

Perkins, Fran D. and Roberta Long. "Author Studies: Profiles in Black." *Teaching K-8* Feb. 1991: 51+.
Suggests teaching strategies for introducing students to a variety of accomplished African American authors. Includes brief reviews of books by each author.

Williams, Helen E. *Books by African-American Authors and Illustrators for Children and Young Adults.* Chicago: American Library Association, 1991.
A bibliography containing over 1,200 briefly annotated entries, this work is divided into four parts: Books for Very Young Children, Books for Intermediate Readers, Books for Young Adult Readers, and Black Illustrators and Their Works.

Publishers of Multicultural Children's Books

Aladdin *(imprint of Macmillan)*
866 Third Ave.
New York, NY 10022
(800) 257-5755

Albert Whitman
5747 W. Howard St.
Nile, IL 60648
(800) 255-7675

American Library Assn.
50 East Huron Street
Chicago, Il 60611
(800) 545-2433

Atheneum *(imprint of Macmillan)*
866 Third Ave.
New York, NY 10022
(800) 257-5755

Beyond Words Publishing
13950 NW Pumpkin Ridge Road
Hillsboro, OR 97123
(800) 284-9673

Bradbury Press (imprint of Macmillan)
866 Third Ave.
New York, NY 10022
(800) 257-5755

Carolrhoda Books
241 First Ave., North
Minneapolis, MN 54401
(800) 328-4929

Chelsea House Publishers
95 Madison Ave.
New York, NY 10016
(800) 848-2665

Children's Book Press
6400 Hollis St.
Emeryville, CA 94608
(800) 999-4650

Childrens Press
5440 N. Cumberland Ave.
Chicago, IL 60656
(800) 621-1115

Clarion Books
215 Park Ave. S
New York, NY 10003
(800) 225-3362

Coward, McCann
200 Madison Ave.
New York, NY 10016
(800) 631-8571

Creative Arts Book Co.
833 Bancroft Way
Berkely, CA 94710
(510) 848-4777

Delacorte
666 Fifth Ave.
New York, NY 10103
(800) 221-4676

Dial (Doubleday)
666 Fifth Ave.
New York, NY 10103
(212) 765-6500
(800) 223-6834, ext. 479

Douglas & McIntyre
1615 Venables St.
Vancouver, BC V5L 2H1 Canada
(604) 254-7191

Facts on File
460 Park Ave., South
New York, NY 10016
(212) 683-2244
(800) 322-8755

Farrar, Straus & Giroux
19 Union Square, West
New York, NY 10003
(212) 741-6900

Four Winds
866 Third Ave.
New York, NY 10022
(800) 257-5755

Franklin Watts
387 Park Ave., South
New York, NY 10016
(212) 686-7070
(800) 672-6672

Fulcrum
350 Indiana St., Suite 350
Golden, CO 80401
(303) 277-1623

Greenwillow Books
105 Madison Ave.
New York, NY 10016
(800) 843-9389

HarperCollins
10 East 53rd St.
New York, NY 10022
(212) 207-7000
(800) 331-3761

Harry N. Abrams
100 Fifth Ave.
New York, NY 10011
(800) 345-1359

Heinemann
361 Hanover St.
Portsmouth, NH 03801
(800) 541-2086

Henry Holt
115 West 18th St.
New York, NY 10011
(212) 886-9200
(800) 247-3912

Highsmith Press
P.O. Box 800C
Highway 106 East
Fort Atkinson, WI 53538
(800) 558-2110

Holiday House
425 Madison Ave.
New York, NY 10017
(212) 688-0085

Hyperion
500 S. Buena Vista
Burbank, CA 91521
(818) 560-1475

James Lorimer
35 Britain St.
Toronto, ON M5A 1R7 Canada
(416) 362-4762

J. B. Lippincott
227 E. Washington Sq.
Philadelphia, PA 19106-3780
(800) 441-4526

Kane/Miller Book Publishers
P.O. Box 529
Brooklyn, NY 11231-0005
(718) 624-5120

Kids Can Press
585 1/2 Bloor St. W.
Toronto, ON M6G 1K5 Canada
(416) 534-6389

Knopf
201 East 50th St.
New York, NY 10022
(212) 572-2103
(800) 733-3000

Lerner Publications
241 First Ave. N.
Minneapolis, MN 55401
(800) 328-4929

Little, Brown & Co.
34 Beacon St.
Boston, MA 02108
(617) 227-0730
(800) 343-9204

Lothrop, Lee & Shepard (Morrow)
1350 Ave. of the Americas
New York, NY 10019
(212) 261-6500
(800) 843-9389

Messner, Julian
190 Sylvan Ave.
Englewood Cliffs, NJ 07632
(201) 592-2464

Northland Publishing
P.O. Box N
Flagstaff, AZ 86002
(602) 774-5251
(800) 346-3257

Orchard Books
387 Park Ave., South
New York, NY 10016
(212) 686-7070
(800) 672-6672

Pantheon Books
201 East 50th St.
New York, NY 10022
(212) 872-8238
(800) 638-6460

Peter Bedrick Books
2112 Broadway, Rm. 318
New York, NY 10023
(212) 496-0751

Philomel Books
200 Madison Ave.
New York, NY 10023
(800) 631-8571

Pocket Books
1230 Ave. of the Americas
New York, NY 10020
(212) 698-7000

Puffin (Penguin)
375 Hudson St.
New York, NY 10014
(212) 366-2000

Putnam
200 Madison Ave.
New York, NY 10016
(212) 951-8400
(800) 631-8571

Schocken Books
201 E. 50th St.
New York, NY 10022
(212) 872-8238

Scholastic
730 Broadway
New York, NY 10003
(212) 505-3000
(800) 392-2179

Silver Burdett Press
190 Sylvan Ave.
Englewood Cliffs, NJ 07632
(800) 843-3464

Steck-Vaughn
P.O. Box 26015
Austin, TX 78755
(800) 531-5015

Sterling Publishing
387 Park Ave. South
New York, NY 10016-8810
(212) 532-7160
(800) 367-9692

Stewart, Tabori, and Chang
575 Broadway
New York, NY 10012
(212) 941-2929

Tundra
1434 Ste. Catherine St. West, #303
Montreal, PQ H3G 1R4 Canada
(514) 932-5434

Cultural Index

Africa, African American

Appalachian

Argentinian

Asia (General), also see specific countries)

Australian

Bahamas

Brazilian

Cambodian

Canadian

Caribbean

Chinese, Chinese American

Egyptian

English

European (General, also see specific countries)

Cultural Index *(cont.)*

Cultural Index (cont.)

Alphabetical Index

Alphabetical Index *(cont.)*

Alphabetical Index (cont.)